The weekend with bearded antique-dealer Claud—and Julia, his
mistress—is spent by

Maggie (once Claud's girlfriend), unstable, sluttish, undeniably
attractive to men, who trails her two latest admirers along with
her;

Norman, a would-be Marxist Liverpuddlian, known as 'Victorian' because that's the style he affects;

and Shebah, an obese anti-semitic Jewish ex-actress.

Norman tries to seduce Julia. Claud in trying to shoot Norman
with an airgun, gets Shebah in the leg and so the chaotic weekend
drags to close with all of them being photographed among the
delphiniums.

*A Weekend With Claud* may leave the reader breathless, but it's
certainly an occasion!

Beryl Bainbridge

# A Weekend with Claud

A Panther Book

A Panther Book

First published in Great Britain by Hutchinson's New Authors
Limited 1967.   Panther edition published 1971.   Copyright ©
Beryl Bainbridge 1967.
*Printed in Great Britain by Richard Clay (The Chaucer Press),
Ltd., Bungay, Suffolk, and published by Panther Books, 3 Upper
James Street, London, W.1*

for my mother

Two people had come to buy a desk.

He had given the date, it wasn't very old, stated the price, no he couldn't go below that figure and agreed with them, yes, it was a lovely desk. And walked away down the long barn towards the open doors in accordance with his practice not to breathe down the necks of potential clients. His customers fell into two categories—the dealers who came to bargain and were not open to influence anyway, and the home lovers mad for possession who needed little encouragement.

He stood in the doorway and looked out at his dying garden. At the stalks of his roses and the ragged trees that had almost lost their leaves, at the few last clumps of marigolds in tubs by the wall.

He had bought the house and the barn for his wife Sally and for their four children six years ago. She had liked the house, she said, and the children put their toys in the rooms and their bicycles in the yard; he bought a dog and a cat and people came in the end not so much to buy his antiques but to see his family and to envy him. Next door to the house was the pub and he made a great show of playing darts there and buying people drinks and they all stood round him in a circle laughing at his jokes. Behind the laughter they were afraid of him as well as envious. On the other side of the house was the girls' boarding school that Maggie, his dear friend Maggie, had gone to as a child, long before he had met her. He had bought the house and moved in before he realised she had gone to school there. Sometimes at night he would lie awake and think how strange it was that Maggie had walked as a child in the Elizabethan gardens beyond his barn. When Sally had left him he telephoned Maggie every night and sometimes two or three times during the day just to talk to someone, just not to be so alone in the house with the rooms strewn with toys and the cradle empty in the bedroom. He wanted her to come to him but she lived up North and she had her own problems, so all she could do was hold the telephone two hundred miles away and listen to him talking. She kept telling him that it would be

all right, that in time it would stop hurting, that from somewhere, someone was coming to love him, just like one of those
songs she was always humming, 'Some day my Prince will
come', though God knows it was Maggie that needed to believe
that, not him. He kept telling her down the black mouth of the
telephone that it was not love he wanted, not that ever again,
but peace. Then Julia had come and tidied away the toys and
put the cradle in the loft, hidden his cigarettes and nursed him
back to health. Most important of all she had allowed him to
love her. Without Julia there would be no house, no barn, no
business, no reason for being alive, no knowledge that it was
possible or necessary to live this way, simply and without torment.

He looked across the stone courtyard to the open door of
the house and saw Julia pass quickly in red slippers, going into
the kitchen to prepare lunch. The glimpse of her filled him
with warmth and a peace that did not pass his understanding.
Under the pale sky and against the wall, pressed close to the
dried stem of the wistaria tree, was his son's pram. A big pram,
an expensive pram with the edge of a white pillow showing at
the hood. He recalled without feeling of any kind that his
other sons, his first-born sons, had slept out their milky days in
a second-hand pram bought for seven-and-six in Camden
Town. A thrifty woman, Sally his wife, in many ways. Bending
her golden head, heavy under its weight of hair, she laid their
children one by one in the cheap carriage on the soiled pillow,
and went melon-hipped and honey-mouthed away from him
into their house. Always away from him.

Behind him in the barn the woman was whispering and he
heard the man say ... 'Yes, but it's just what we visualised' ...
and he moved his head because he did not care at that moment
to know what it was other people visualised. It was sufficient
to stand like a figure in a painting in a half-open doorway,
allowing a little of the interior to be glimpsed but leaving the
landscape ahead entirely to the imagination. He slid his hand
into the opening of his check shirt and caressed his breast. For
comfort and from habit he massaged his skin with gentleness.
He did not turn round or withdraw his hand when the man
said just behind him:

'Well, Mr White, my wife and I have decided to take the

desk.'

Then he did turn round, away from the garden's decline, and narrowed his eyes to adjust them to his customer's expression, which was an open one and mixed with pleasure, for the decision made and the desk he was soon to own and use, to set in his house somewhere among his other possessions in which he might or might not find delight.

The wife was opening drawers and rummaging with her hands inside the cool interiors. Her fingers searched in the narrow darkness fretfully, and found something.

'Oh look,' she cried out with wonder, feeling the evidence first and then seeing it, 'a photograph and a letter.'

The letter and the photograph she held aloft in her greedy fingers and waved about in the air.

'Ah,' said Claude, 'yes, I'm afraid I put them there and forgot, only a few weeks ago.' Which was the truth, only not altogether forgotten. He moved regretfully towards her, to her scarlet mouth open in disappointment, to her female face misted with powder, and allowed himself to lose his detachment and smile at her winningly, saying: 'So sorry, my dear, it's nothing more historical than a letter written me by a friend. It's not much of a find. You know, in all my years in the antique business I've yet to come across anything of real significance.'

All the time his own fingers were held up to hers, as if they reached together to pluck an identical sprig of mimosa, and behind them the husband said, clearing an obstruction in his throat:

'Oh, come on now, Betty, give Mr White his letter. We really must be moving.'

The dictates of polite behaviour overlaid the barn like a mantle. Claud would have liked to snatch the letter still held in her on-high grasp and flick her meanly across the bridge of her little tilted nose, there where the powder grains lay like pollen on her skin. He was forced to wait until her arm came down at last, and she handed him his letter, her mouth alone betraying a pouting obstinacy.

'Do come and meet Julia,' said Claud, folding his letter and putting it and the photograph in the breast pocket of his shirt, patting them flat with the tips of thanksgiving fingers. Without waiting for a reply to his invitation he led the way out of the barn and across the yard into the house. His hand stayed at his breast, fingers pinned like a brooch to the pocket of his shirt. Julia at the stove looked up and smiled mildly at their entrance. The red slippers on her small feet made her appear young. She had been peeling potatoes and also preparing the child's nappies for washing. The thoroughness with which she did everything meant that most ordinary household tasks took her far longer than was necessary. The diapers had been soaking all night and were now half-washed preparatory to being boiled and washed yet again. They lay modestly in a blue polythene bucket by the sink and emitted no smell at all. 'Coffee,' said Claud, not unkindly, though he knew this would delay Julia even further and would cause her to become irritable later in the day.

'You are naughty, Claud,' she would scold. 'I've so much to do and you know how I hate getting behind my schedule.'

'What a charming kitchen,' said the woman Betty. She peered with exaggerated interest at the two china heads, two rustic sweethearts with apple cheeks laid against each other, attached to the wall. 'Oh, how sweet. Look, Stanley, aren't they sweet?' In looking she kicked the polythene bucket beside the sink and a small drop of cold water spilled on to her foot. 'Oh how clumsy, I'm sorry.' And stood there whilst Claud knelt at her feet and patted her shoe dry with a dishcloth. 'Oh, you really shouldn't bother,' she said, confused and looking over his head first at Julia and then at Stanley. Kneeling as he was, Claud felt the photograph in his pocket stiff against his skin, and beneath that his heart beating, beating rather rapidly with the effort of stooping.

It did not seem a long time ago since he was young, or younger, since he had been two stones lighter, since his wife had gone away. She had walked so deliberately out of the door, without even a coat, and surely she would not leave without a coat, and he had followed her down the street to the bridge and then stopped and watched her walk away from him over the river, her hands by her sides. He had remembered that when he first met her it had been by a river and she had been sitting in the grass in a dress with a collar that did not quite fit, and he had thought, looking at her face, and the shadows of leaves that dappled her skin, I will make you my wife.

It was not so much love at first sight as the decision of a man who knew a beautiful thing when he saw it and wanted to own it. For which he had paid not in money but in pain, because he found there was no way of making her love him and no way of putting her out of his heart or his mind. She had moved through their life together completely self-contained, without emotion, without anger or compassion. Nothing he had done had reached her. The pain of this discovery at first resembled a length of elastic stretched tight across his whole personality. If he relaxed for a moment and allowed himself to dwell on her apathy towards him it snapped loose and bruised him violently. After a time the hurt slackened and he only ached. He had been so ill for a year following her departure over the bridge, out of his reach, that he had not been aware of the gradual accumulation of flesh. It had been almost a surprise to find himself finally so large and bulky in his person. Julia thought it was the drink. Probably it was, but privately he believed it was the body's way of protecting itself against being beautiful ever again. There was a time, after all, to cease being beautiful and a time to cease being young, and with him it had been when his wife left him. If he had been less weak he might have been able to keep the children, which like her coat she had not bothered to take with her, but he had gone into hospital and they had been taken away. It was something he tried, and failed, not to think about.

He rose slowly with the cloth in his hand and smiled at Betty. He had rather small white teeth between pink lips set in his crisp beard.

'Thank you,' she said, looking past him at her husband.

Julia had begun to boil water for the coffee. 'Only Nescafé I'm afraid,' and paused, watching Claud as if half expecting he would say it would not do. But he chose not to hear the enquiry in her voice and was opening a box that stood on the kitchen table, packed full of china that he had bought earlier that morning.

Stanley was left standing in the doorway without contact. He had the feeling that if he spoke he would receive no reply. However, he could not keep silent. 'Anything very interesting, old man?' and quickly, to fill the void in which Claud went on unwrapping plates: 'Shall I make out a cheque for the desk now, Mr White?'

Claud had rolled up the sleeves on his check shirt. His forearms were squat and hairless, elbow-deep in newspapers. 'Yes, if you like.' At the corner of his mouth he had sucked in a tendril of beard. There was no room to write on the table and the only other surface, the draining board, was wet with soapy water, so that the man was forced to hold his cheque book high against the wall. He found his eyes level with the two china heads, with the two rosy mouths. He half turned his head to look at his wife and in doing so his hand slipped and his book fell to the floor beside the polythene bucket. His half-completed signature blurred. 'Damn,' he said, bending to retrieve it and flapping it about in the air.

'It's quite all right,' said Claud, 'don't bother to write a fresh one.'

He did not look up and the cheque lay on the table among the newspapers with its tear-stained name.

Outside in the yard the baby woke under the sky and began to make small sounds of distress or hunger, and Julia said: 'Oh, Claud darling, do get him,' bringing back memories of other babies crying in another pram who were not picked up until somebody was ready and who were none the worse for it.

'Julia, look at these, aren't they nice?' Claud held up one of the plates for her inspection.

'Yes, they are nice.' Head down, her spectacles misty from the steam of the coffee now in the cups, Julia put the sugar bowl on the table amid the papers. Also a tin of biscuits.

'Do sit down,' said Claud to Betty, and he gathered up quantities of newspaper and dropped them on to the kitchen floor. The cheque went too. Stanley saw it float under the table and come to rest against the leg of a stool, but he said nothing.

'Shall I get the baby?' asked Betty of Julia who was getting spoons from a drawer.

'No, leave him.' Claud took her elbow and sat her down on a stool.

She did not like to look at him directly. She sensed that he was hostile towards her and yet the moist mouth smiled.

'I bought these plates from a woman in the next village,' said Claud. 'I constantly buy for money things that people no longer value. When I was younger I could hardly bear to part with anything I bought. Now I'm not so foolish.'

'Have you many things that you purchased when you first started in the business?' asked Stanley, thrusting his fist into the pocket of his trousers. It was a damn fine desk and a damn fine house, but he didn't know how to take this fellow. He couldn't explain it, but the blighter seemed so hostile. And it had been his suggestion that they stay for coffee.

'No,' said Claud. 'I had, but my wife took everything when she left.'

'Oh.'

Betty sat quite still on her stool at the table and Julia went out of the kitchen in her little red slippers, out into the yard, and the crying of the child suddenly ceased. Presently they heard her come into the passage and go up the stairs.

'My little lamb, my little honey love, Mummy's little honey take.'

A door upstairs closed and clipped short the sweet words, the honey melody.

'Have you ever thought, man,' said Claud, though he was looking into the face of Betty, 'how eatable are the words of endearment, how full of sugar? There's a very good reason for it of course.'

'Oh, how's that?' In spite of himself, Stanley put the question. He sat down at the table opposite his wife and stirred his coffee.

'Simple, man. The body needs sugar, it's the energy source. At birth a child undergoes six hours of hunger, sometimes much more. But six hours is the maximum before the body experiences actual starvation.'

'Really.' Betty had never had children. They had tried but had been unsuccessful.

'Oh, it's perfectly true. Then the child starts crying, crying because it's starving, and the mother takes over, either with the breast or a bottle.'

The man felt uneasy at the use of the word breast. He had a terrifying image of himself laid against the huge and purple nipple of his mother. Saliva gathered in his mouth. He glanced at the tailored front of his wife's costume and was aware of Claud saying . . .

'A child that is denied food when it cries is also denied love, I reckon. The withholding of food by the mother object is a withholding of love. And it doesn't just stop there, you know.

Most mentally disturbed adults crave sugar. You know, sweets and sugary drinks, all the fattening things.' He crumpled a piece of newspaper between his fingers and rolled it into a ball. 'They've done some extremely interesting experiments in America, you know. They put three mental patients into a room with two doctors and they gave them the usual shock treatment to the mid-brain. Then they put all sorts of candies and sweets in front of the poor devils and watched them eat. Suddenly they removed all the food out of reach, very swiftly, and the first patient screamed—For God's sake give us more love—and the second said to the doctor—Please, Mother—and held out his hands.' He opened his own hands in illustration and the ball of newspaper dropped to the floor. There was a silence in the kitchen.

The man Stanley held his cup in his two palms and heard his wife ask in a high foolish voice: 'But what about the third man, the third patient? What did he say?'

'I really don't remember, my dear.'

'Do you really believe in all this neurotic nonsense?' Stanley shook his head as if to clear away doubts, but the feeling of irritation persisted. He was surprised at the loudness of his own voice. There was something about this fellow White that made you feel he was being personally vindictive. And he'd damn well let his own child cry long enough out there in the garden. If it was his child.

'Oh, I do. There's a great deal in it. Else why should you at this moment feel such resentment? We all suffer from the same sense of loss.'

A laugh, however contemptuous, did not seem adequate, so Stanley said nothing and sweat accumulated under the armpits of his striped and newly laundered shirt.

'You know that's why you girls like having your breasts sucked. You know instinctively you are giving the man both food and love.' Claud, eyes tender and amused, leaned forward and put his arm around Betty's shoulders and shook her. 'It's true, isn't it, girl? It's the truth, isn't it?'

She was consumed with embarrassment and excitement. It was as if he had shown her a pack of obscene photographs in the normality of her own living room. His head was so close to hers that the curling strands of beard caressed her cheek, that his breath touched her skin. She saw that Stanley's face appeared blurred in the little room, that his mouth was open. On his hand he wore a ring given him by his father, a gold ring with a dull green stone. She kept her eyes focussed on this, this hard substance that linked her to all their shared memories, because she felt that if she looked away the link would be broken and she would make some wanton remark to this bearded man with his talk of breasts and his large arm so protectively about her shoulders. And there was a recollection in her mind that came quite unbidden, of herself as a child in a back room with a mahogany sideboard with two drawers, and of her mother leaving her alone in the house for some mis-demeanour, something wrong, and she had opened the right-hand drawer of the sideboard and found a bag of sweets and eaten them one by one, boiled sweets as round and hard as the stone in Stanley's ring. She wondered if the woman Julia gave her breasts to both the baby and the bearded man, if she called him her honey lamb and dropped milk into his full mouth. Her thoughts only heightened her helplessness. She leant her head against Claud's shoulder and stared at Stanley's hand which moved and gripped the edge of the table, and then he laughed, which freed her, so that she sat upright.

'It's been most interesting,' said her husband, his face still split with some kind of elation, 'but it's time we were moving. It certainly is time.' He stood up and shook himself more securely into the jacket of his good grey suit, and heard the loose change jingle in his pocket. And was at once wholly himself and solid again, and more than a little amused with this conversation in a kitchen with a man who had lost his wife and who imagined that men took seriously all this talk of babyhood and women's chests.

Julia came back into the room in her red slippers, bringing with her a smell of talcum powder. She was no longer pale or so downcast; her lips and cheeks seemed to have filled out and gathered colour from the child. 'I'm sorry to have been so long,' she said, though she knew it was possible her absence had been scarcely noticed. She made an affected gesture with her rather long fingers: 'The baby, you know.'

'They've bought the desk, the one I picked up in Leeds,' said Claud, rising from the table and lifting the pile of newly acquired plates and carrying them to the sink.

'Oh, how nice.' Julia bent and began collecting newspapers from the floor.

'My wife had a bit of a disappointment, though,' said Stanley, watching his cheque swept up with the rest of the debris. 'She found a letter and a photograph in the desk but they belonged to Mr White.'

'I did think it was at least an old will or a treasure map,' said Betty.

Claud was putting detergent into the bowl in the sink and running hot water. Through the steam he said: 'Instead of which it was merely an old letter of Maggie's and a photograph I took in the garden that weekend last summer.'

'Oh, that one.' It was hard to tell how Julia meant that. 'Where is it?'

'In my top pocket.'

She put her slim hand into his breast pocket and drew out the photograph and looked at it. 'It seems such a long time ago. Poor dear Shebah,' and placed it down on the table.

Stanley looked at it, at the three figures seated on the grass, a man a little to one side, another in the foreground and a girl between them. Behind them in a chair was an old woman with a bandage round her leg. It was not a very good photograph, but he looked at the face of the girl and said 'Who's that?' half thinking it might be the missing wife gone with all the furniture and small blame to her by the sound of it.

'It's a friend of Claud's, someone very dear to him,' Julia said with calmness, touching the photograph gently with the tips of her fingers, 'He's known her for years, haven't you, Claud?'

'Yes, for years.'

Which was the truth. For years and for years he had known her. He and Sally had two rooms and three children when he had first met Maggie. She lived up the Heath end of Parliament Hill and they lived at the bottom. Sometimes she baby-sat for them, once she cut Sally's hair; she told him about Joseph the student she was in love with back home in Liverpool, who wasn't in love with her. In the secure position of one who knew the pain of unrequited love he advised her to forget Joseph. 'But I can't,' she told him, 'I have to marry him. I will marry him, there's no other way unless he could die.' In the end she had her way, Joseph being healthy, and in time after the children were born he went away and left her. Her next lover had proved no more adequate at loving her in the way she desired—how could he?—and she had been left alone again. Always Maggie brought her lovers to be seen by him. He hadn't liked Joseph and he hadn't cared for Billie; the last one, Edward, the much-needed Edward, she had brought to him last summer, along with her comrade Victorian Norman and her friend Shebah.

He looked down at the plates in the sink and lapped water over the painted flowers. Behind him the man Stanley picked up the photograph, looking again at the blurred features of the girl. It was as if he held the camera, as if he were about to click the shutter out there in last summer's garden; the lens of his eye blinked and recorded her image, her dark mouth, her white cheeks, her slightly smiling eyes looking straight into his. . . .

Maggie

I don't know if I've had a nice time or not, though I suppose that wasn't the object of the exercise. Anyway it's settled now, though it may be foolish to imagine anything really settled. This morning when I first got up, before the shooting of Shebah, I felt so clean and wide awake. Now I feel tired and would like a bath. I could have one but it would mean walking away from them down the garden and into the house, and Edward would follow in case I was being molested by Claud, so it's not worth it. When we arrived yesterday, the four of us, and the children, I shouted very loudly in the street outside so as not to sound nervous. I was not confident about all the luggage we had brought, because it looked as if we had come for a month, not a night and a day and a morning. There were the children's clothes for bed and extra jumpers in case it turned colder, and some cars for Boy and a doll for my girl, and a special little case of clothes for the doll, who is called Winnie. And Edward's case with shaving things and my nightie, though I don't often wear one. I just didn't want to wander round the house all night stark naked. Victorian Norman had a haversack because he is going straight up North afterwards and will camp on the way, and Shebah had her usual bag full of letters and lawsuits and cuttings from the *Observer*. We came Indian file, partly because the pavement was narrow and partly because we each wanted to look self-effacing and less in numbers. We did look interesting in a sort of way, and I felt a bit proud and a bit ashamed of us all. I don't seem to have grown used, deep down, to having come so far from my childhood environment. Even living in London seems odd, let alone being almost divorced and owning children and having funny friends. Not funny really, not in the laughable sense, though Shebah could be defined so, if she was just looked at. She's not talking now, which makes her look different, clumsy, because most of Shebah is how she throws up her plump arms so that the yellow bangles slither down, and all the words she uses. Just now she sits on a white cane chair, pouting, eyes closed behind her glasses. She wanted to sit on the grass (too damp) because she appreciates the daisies; like me she's probably thinking inside how they approach most closely to the image of herself, little and pretty and white.

I don't really, it's just that I've trained my mind to think these thoughts, and I've found lately that maybe I haven't an image at all. Or if I have it's blurred. Coming here on the bus I had an image of myself as a chatterer, with—Oh, that's a lovely house, and—Oh, what a super house—at least I said all that because Victorian Norman never said a word, just stared out of the window, and I did want us to sound as if we were animated. Edward sat in front with Boy and it meant I could lean forward and put my hand on his neck and I felt happy making contact, because I thought it looked as if we had been married for years and me still adored.

I mean I feel fairly certain I am still adored but then I've only known him a little while and he doesn't know me very well. I met him at a party and I always make an impact at first meeting, that is if the person involved is lost enough or odd enough or something. At least it's always been like that before. Edward at the moment seems to be the exception and he just might marry me if I'm nice enough long enough. And I just have to be this time, because of the baby not yet born, and that's partly why we all came here this weekend: for me to make Edward the father of the baby. I've never been so cunning before. Never. It's not really such a mean trick to play on anyone, well not Edward, because he loves children so much and particularly mine and Boy worships him. All the way here on the bus he sat on Edward's knee and chatted to him and Edward held him close and Shebah passed round sweeties which we took because she never takes no for an answer, just keeps on delving into her bag and thrusting them at us.

I thought I knew the road. I had been on the Green Line bus several times when I used to go to school here, but it was only like in those cowboy films when there seem a lot of Indians falling off horses, when it's only the same Indian, and I kept thinking I knew the next bend in the road, only I didn't after all; it was just like a thousand other roads bordered with green hedges and ribboned with grass and the same old tree bending down.

I only remember one ride to school, in the dark, the first term, with my hair waved permanently, and a grey school coat that had the same texture as my head, harsh and hairy. The bus turned off the road into a drive, and there were great dark trees and a notice board showing faintly, and someone said we were there. We ate egg on toast in a basement that might have been a dungeon, and there were long loaves of bread with wet insides, and most of the girls seemed elderly and lit cigarettes after the meal. One had little yellow curls on both sides of her ears and a clever amused expression, and after she yawned she said: 'My God, I'm tired.' Then we walked in the dark outside and under some trees and through a door that had horses' hooves nailed up all over it, and up some stone steps into a room with three beds. The girl with the clever face said I had better make my bed, and another girl came in with a full face and long lobes to her ears and started to eat an onion. I turned my back and fiddled with my bedding and looked at the tapes my mother had sewn on the blankets with my name on, and water came into the back of my eyes because I did not know how to make a bed, and I felt foolish and sad and not at all beautiful. I wasn't at all beautiful but every day at the same time I told myself (no, told God)—Please make me beautiful—and that made my inside feel better. But there had been so many new things all that day, and in the rain a man with a homburg hat had said I was intelligent, that I had omitted to tell God, so that I now felt just what I was, squat and shabby and plain. The tears on my cheeks were for that mainly, though I would have liked to make my bed up properly. In the end I had to turn round and the onion-eater said. 'Aren't you the girl that's had no schooling?' in a funny sprawled voice, a South African take-me-back-to-the-old-Transvaal voice, and I said, 'Yes.' It was easier than saying I had not got a bed of my own at home and that I slept with my mother, and that she always made the bed anyway, and that my brother slept with my father. There were two empty bedrooms as well and we all slept without nightclothes, except my father, who wore cream combinations. If there had ever been a fire God help us, we would all have had to burn rather than come down a ladder so unprepared, and if one of us went to the lavatory in the middle of the night, Father would shout out: 'Many there, luv?' This girl, who was later quite nice, and who used to break into the Prince Igor dances at the drop of a hat, proving to me how lucky I was in possessing sensitivity, seeing that I was thinner than her but would have died rather than dance anything and show my muscular calves, helped me to make the bed, whilst the other girl lay back more amused than ever, and I thought I had better worry tomorrow about the misunderstanding about my former expensive education.

I should have shown Shebah the school. I expect she would have called me a bloody rotten swine for having all that luxury and beauty around me, but underneath she would have been impressed.

There's very little about the schooldays that I remember now, except the snow coming down one winter term when we went on a Sunday morning to church, and the flakes were like daisies and the Salvation Army band were playing 'The Sea of Love is Rolling In', and though it was a bit like a Christmas card I did feel like crying or did cry, only it was I think mostly that moments like that always move me off the idea of how beautiful I was (am) and I get all lost and puny and dwindle right down to almost nothing. I might have felt like that because whilst the band played 'The Sea of Love Comes Rolling In' the flakes of snow were coming down from a great height and getting lost underfoot. Anyway I remember the morning for that reason and because later in church I did not kneel down quick enough and Matron behind tapped me with her umbrella, and I almost, not quite, contemplated turning round and striking her. Not that I minded too much the umbrella but that I was lost watching the vicar, and was alternating between thinking he was Rochester and I was Jane Eyre (what, leave Ferndale and all that I hold most dear?) and the idea of him and me going down on the *Titanic* together, with the violins playing, and Matron spoilt it all.

I haven't even told Edward I went to school here, or about the vicar. If I sat up now he would be watching me. He is watching me. He's also looking to see how close Victorian Norman is to my leg. That's because last night he stood at the top of the stairs and watched Norman and I leaning on each other. We were really laughing, though I was crying. Norman has got an awful laugh. A sort of current of air blown out of some horse with flaring nostrils, and sucked in again.

When I first heard it I was interviewing him about a room in our house in Morpeth Street. There was only me living there then and Billy the Wild Colonial Boy and Miss Evans the hair remover, who pretended she didn't live there and changed into mackintosh and gumboots when she returned from work at the end of the day, and carried a torch. She did not like to use the light switches in case she got a shock, which was being a bit over-cautious, but then her electrolysis career had probably unnerved her. Anna or Brenny or someone said they knew a man who would be suitable to live in the house, as he was clean and quiet and did not like meeting people, and I did need the money, so I said he could come round and I'd talk to him.

He does not really look so odd now, propped on one elbow, digging at the grass with bony fingers, and his frown is not displeasure but just that he's thinking over the events of last night. When I opened the door to him at our first meeting he was small and Victorian and had straight-down trousers without a turn-up when everybody else had turn-ups, and a high collar round his throat, with rounded edges like the ones my father wore, and under the flat peaked cap a face like the German prisoner of war I knew as a child, eyes turned down at the corners, and a nose with wide nostrils, and a long thin upper lip. I hadn't remembered the German for a long time, and whilst I began to do so Norman walked past me into the hall and like a very old film winding jerkily, ducked his head, removed his cap, patted his hair, slapped his cap between his hands and gave his laugh. Only I did not hear the laugh properly that first time because I was thinking of where I used to meet the German prisoner, under the pale beech leaves by the pinewoods, and remembering the long gummy strands that spiders spun and slung from tree to tree, and the way they caught in my hair, and the sound a pheasant made rising up from the ground with a great surge of wings, and I suppose that was Norman laughing.

There was a fire in my living room, which was a nice room, with Sicilian lions with tongues sticking out wallpapered all along one side, and a brass bed and the piano and two samovars and the head of a moose with a paper garland twisted round its horns, and the fire burning, and I felt very like a landlady, which I was, and very formal. I started to say that I did like to be quiet, but he did not stop at a distance to listen, but advanced closer and closer, neck stuck out like a tortoise above the wing collar, head inclined slightly, till we were nose to nose, and he squinted at my mouth, and my skirt began to catch fire. O-Ho, I thought, this is a right one all right, and on the thought was spun round with two hands low on my hips, and then held with one hand whilst he beat at my bottom with his flat check cap. After he came to live in the house he said he couldn't believe his luck, me catching fire like that, and I said it was no wonder and did he always have to talk to one so intensely. He said he had wax in both ears and had to lip read to understand properly and that was why he moved so near. I did once get him to have the wax cleaned out, but he suffered terribly for weeks from all the cups rattling in the Kardomah, and the machines at work, and I had to buy him ear-plugs till the wax re-formed.

He's looking at me now, a little groove at the top of his nose, and he's looking sad in his blue eyes. There, we met for an instant, and I don't feel so cheerful any more, though it's only temporary. We did decide some time ago to treat life as a comedy, applaud loudly each fresh banana skin fall, bear in mind constantly that emotions are transient. This time, for the first time, we won't be able to go over this weekend with care, verbally smoothing the distress into recognisable symbols. We won't be able to reiterate till we have absorbed without possibility of forgetfulness every word, every inflection, every sentence, that Shebah uttered from the moment of arrival to the time the pellet hit her in the leg, and afterwards. This time we won't because Norman will be going back up North and I'll be returning to the lightness of the new southern flat with the wide white window sills. This time we won't, because it's all so final, so serious. A crusade to end all crusades, Norman terms it. I don't really think it's that serious. To find a father for a child. Norman was going to tell me what he thought about Edward, whether he thought he was suitable, but we haven't really discussed it. I think Edward will be all right. He is, after all, the reflection of the tenderness I bear for myself. It is always ourselves we love.

Shebah has just moved one plump hand down reproachfully to touch her bandaged leg. It is as if one of the statues has stirred. In an instant she will groan and then say something. Victorian Norman closes his eyes, waiting. There, she speaks ... 'What's the bloody swine up to now?'

Edward says pleasantly, taking the opportunity to clear his throat. 'Getting ready to take us to the bus.'

The figure all in black falls back into the chair. A ladder moves swifter than the eye can follow up the apricot stocking. What was it she said last night, round the kitchen table, rosered bottom lip drooping, eyes assuming a childishness she has never lost...? 'There is a moment when everything is too late.' Claud had bent low over the cottage pie, in sympathy, short fingers supporting his fierce head.

'Aah, dear Shebah ... dear Shebah.'

Passively Julia went on eating.

'Late for what?' Edward looked at her, hands searching in his pockets for the cigarettes he wanted.

Yesterday, going through the door into the shop, Claud held out arms so wide that there was no way to go but into them. The gold beard brushed my half-open mouth, behind the smooth, vast perfectly hairless chest, a heart palpitated. Within the now-closed arms, pressed against the dilating blood machine, through half-shut eyes and strands of hair, I saw the shop. The tables of china and ornaments, the ceiling hung with lamps, the hamster cage, a drawing that I'd done two years ago pinned on a wall, a dozen mirrors reflecting a hundred glitterings and the bland face of Julia, gentle, smiling, waiting for a greeting. At the moment of penetration into the shop, or partial penetration, because our embrace had piled the others into a neat heap behind, Victorian Norman trod on the foot of Shebah, the exposed foot in the openwork sandal. The doorbell continued to ring and over it Sheba swore.

'Man,' said Claud, holding Edward by the fingers, 'good to see you.' One hand touched his own naked nipple under the open shirt, the eyes became obliterated in the creases of a smile. Crooning he took Shebah forward, and then Julia said the right things, the nice things, and we were through the shop, into the hall and going up the open staircase to the living room above. A wooden angel tethered to the wall held praying hands above Shebah's Napoleonic pigtail.

'Oh my God,' she breathed.

I wanted to hug Edward, I wanted to stand on tiptoe and pirouette on the Indian carpet and show him everything at once, but I was torn by wanting to show Shebah and Victorian Norman too. I pointed fingers quickly in all directions: the jade for Shebah, the Boucher nudes for Norman, and I brought my hand round past the piano and the glass and the silver and the gold in a circle back to myself, meaning for Edward, who wasn't watching, all this and me too. Claud was watching and he knew what I meant and I nearly shouted with laughter, though again I might have felt like crying. All this emotion is, as Shebah would put it, so wearying. So like my papa am I, ready to weep at 'Silver Threads Among the Gold', and giving two-shilling pieces to the boys in blue during the late last war, and maybe rather charming now with my brown hair and full mouth and not so old, but what when I'm lately young, and the lines criss-crossing like a map in all directions under the eyes, and the little lanes going nowhere across the brow, meditation, bewilderment, lack of oil?

Shebah has a face that is old, but it's almost as if she is in disguise, when she is not talking, which is not often. First the moustache and the glasses, and the black hat with the pigtail attached, and the bags bulging with last decade's letters, and a photograph of her father in a little gilt frame, standing in a road going somewhere, with a waxy moustache and a secret Hebrew smile, showing nothing. That and the other photograph not often shown, but carried always in her bag (in case of what situation?), of herself, bosoms riding some little impudent waves, beside a promenade, black curls wind-blown, God knows how many outings ago.

Upstairs in Claud's room there was so much to look at and touch that we did not have to talk for a little while. I went through with Julia into a bedroom and she said ... 'This is for you and Edward, I hope you like it' ... as if I had not been there before, which in a way I had not. Pink-washed walls and a china cherub on a shelf above the bedhead, and another with dimpled arms and a pot belly holding up a lamp bulb. Outside the window combustion sounds as cars drove along the highway under a blue sky. Julia smoothed down her hair, only a habit, and behind the glasses the eyes were mild, kind, clear, healthy.

'How are things? You look so well. It's unbelievable.'

I had to look then into the blotched mirror on the wall to make sure I did. 'I feel marvellous,' I told her, looking at the image of my face. 'It's a feeling of being alive, Julia.'

I did mean it. I do mean it, I think I do. There was loud

laughter coming from the living room adjacent. Possibly Claud and Victorian Norman running suggestive fingers across the painting of the nude girl above the fireplace. I looked for Edward and found him in the room that the children were to sleep in, sitting on a top bunk, trying to mend a car for Boy. Worried, stiff little bottom curved in denim shorts, Boy asked ... 'I heard dogs, where are they?'

Edward put the car down on the blue blanket. 'Try that, Boy,' he said.

Over the heads of the children we looked at each other, and I tried to be happy and failed. The eyes were blue, only tighter, more like flowers, than those others, the bigger paler eyes I had looked into across the same distance, only three weeks earlier. This face was more patient, more human, more like a real face, though I don't know if I am being fair. If I think at all about Billie's face or about Billie, I think of a large hearty boy, a buffoon with a wide womanish expression, who moved with clumsiness exaggerated, because the body was not clumsy but adroit, smooth, knowing just where it wanted to go, to walk, to lie down in green pastures. When he spoke he inclined his head diffidently, as if he didn't know how clearly, how specifically, with what charm he would say ... 'Really, how well you understand' ... and then the laugh, the patter, the carefully modulated tone, and one muscular hand (blond hairs thick across the knuckle bones) rubbing ruefully the back of his neck, a big neck, a man's neck.

Victorian Norman has hands with hair on them, but the thumbs are thin and long.

Billie's were fat pads of flesh swelling out in otherwise small hands; they dug into the mohair skirt I wore for the cocktail party my mother gave, before my father died. I sat on a kitchen chair, low on the ground, and Billie knelt with hands round my waist and said with the drink, trying to be sincere: 'I love you ... I do love you, little one.' And my father passing through into the scullery to wash yet more glasses, half spun on tiny feet, face white, as if to say ... 'God knows I can't make head nor tail of this.' My mother came in then with another man, and she was less desperate than my father, more bothered about what people might think, and she mouthed 'Get up' and then laughed immoderately. Billie (a name for a comedian, a funny thing happened to me the other night) was on his feet ... 'How very nice you look.'

Father, a figure painted by Roault with staring eyes, the Christmas singer of 'Lily of Laguna', once sung in knicker-bockers with just such hostility in his gaze, repassed without a word. 'Chickie', he might have said, but he did not.

My mother said later that she knew then that things were very serious between Billie and me, which was perceptive of her because I didn't know. I was still in love with Joseph, my lawful husband, who had introduced me to Billie in the first place and encouraged us to go about together, all of us being so artistic and unconventional and above things like jealousy and fidelity.

Mrs Ryan looked after the children that morning, as she did the night Billie and I first went out together. A charity concert and a large lady singing 'O Rose Marie I love You', and then I was sick all over Billie's trousers, and such great convulsions of the stomach, and the noise of me being sick echoing all long the stone corridor.

Was I happy? Was it me? Victorian Norman claims he knows me. Impossible to have knowledge of someone based on two years of sitting in a kitchen endlessly talking ... talking. What about all the years before that, the foundling years, the baby years? Little lamb, who made thee? What about all that time I worked in the theatre, and the producer playing on a piano over and over, because it was the only thing he could play and indulge his lyrical mind, 'Sheep May Safely Graze', may safely, may safely ... and so on until Joseph my husband-to-be appeared from the wings and called my name. I refuse to think that far back; that way, as Shebah would say, madness lies. And the time working in Scotland again with the piano-playing producer, the Catholic Saint with the handkerchiefs saturated in eau-de-Cologne (he loses more converts to the Faith than the Inquisition) and hiring a car to go a ride into the country so as to be bona-fide travellers and get some whisky in the cold Sunday afternoon. How well I talked, how intelligent I was. Ending in a barren field, trees shaking in blustering wind against a thick white sky, lurching in step under the producer's duffel coat, and Madame Blanche, the Infanta of Navarre of next week's production (a princess of beauty and dignity), a tubby bundled woman with mascara mingling with her tears, standing on the little bridge of Kerriemur, trying to learn her lines and shaking disappointed hands. I had a flat in a tenement, a lovely flat, with a tram-line running right down the street outside my window, and a fire lit in the grate by my landlady each night. And all that business of becoming a Catholic.

The three things that may be thought necessary to commit sin. Full knowledge, full consent and grave matter. Even now the last condition strikes chill to my heart. Lean forward in a passion of grief, hitting the breastbone with contrition, watch the black smoke from the candles ... through my fault, my fault, my most grievous.

Shebah said something then, but I didn't hear. Because of her leg, because of her accident, which was only an accident in that Claud had not intended to shoot her but someone else, what she said was probably brutal.

'You disgust me,' she may have said. Her egotism is such that she believes that Claud did indeed aim at her. 'I despise you, you disgust me' ... 'I disgust myself', her heart may have echoed. 'I despise myself.' It is only ourselves we have charity enough to find truly disgusting.

Shebah has behaved well, coming here, that is. Norman refused to travel with her, but he put her on the London train and without compassion walked away in the middle of her hand-waving and her sobbing, white scarf a-fluttering. She has always said that she would never go on a train because of sitting with all the scum, and yet the idea of travel appeals to her. At one time we discussed the possibility of her perhaps making a permanent life for herself on the railways, at night, when she would not see so many people. 'Living is what gets me down, darling, but if I could just move about sitting down, and just see things through windows without being observed, it would be splendid.'

Actually she desires people like some people desire money or fame. Through them she transcends her ageing body (sixty or more years) and constantly moves through crowds, watching for the sideways glance, half fearing, half revelling in the eyes that turn towards her with their expressions of surprise, dismay, recognition, and on a bad day, rejection. Her conception of herself, the young bosoms bobbing on the waves, the plump shoulders touched by the sea at Blackpool, the too clever girl of forty years ago, never wavers entirely. With Norman and me it is rock strong, but she finds an exquisite masochism in risking consciousness of her limitations, her downy lip, her myopic eyes behind the double lenses, the uniform of black skirt and jumper, worn, it would seem, to confirm her conviction about those other rotten bloody swines with their cars and their villas, dressed to kill. Where were you educated? 'The University of Life, darling.' Her real and imaginary tormentors, real in that they do exist, the dressed ones, the owners of cars, though imaginary in that they are unaware of her, are always female.

'If I really bothered, darling, if I really cared to dress, darling, they'd kill me with their jealousy. Oh God,' the smooth arms fly upward appealing to heaven, then hang downwards, palms open, as if to say, Here I am without guile, without trappings, the yellow and green bangles slide to rest on the arthritic wrist bones, 'they'd smother me with their bloody rotten jealousy.'

To the men she is more generous. The worn lipstick in her bag, sticky at the edges, is taken out and colour placed on the bottom lip, the voluptuary lower lip, and above the mouth incredibly the nose comes forth chiselled and disciplined, a delicate pink suffusing the vomer of the nostrils. After this she will talk. It is a verbal seduction. The miasma of words begins in the eyes, they spit out through the ruined mouth, and the shoulders and the arms and the hands take part in the performance. Because it is a performance. Only the short legs (bent at and knees at this moment) look out of place. They are so Edwardian, so shapely, not a vein, not a hair blemishes the whiteness of the full calves. The bandage round her ankle she regards as a stigmata ... ('2,000,000 of my people in the gas ovens, darling'). I wish I had learned about Jews before I became a Catholic. Shebah gets such comfort out of all the persecution.

The day before I married, for I did get married, I rode a bicycle through the village, trying to find a priest to whom I could make a confession. There was mist rising up from the fields and a locked church door and some dead flowers in the porch. So that the next day, the wedding morn, dressed in cream and beads and crowned with a hat of flowers, April flowers, I moved up the aisle in a state of sin, watched by the pews of non-believing guests, to join my atheist bridegroom with the bowed bearded head, and two lines of Latin later I was no longer a miss, or a nymphet of the pinewoods, but a married woman to all intents.

Did I go through floods for this, to lie here on the grass staring up at a sky, white (not blue because I am looking directly at the sun), and really having learnt nothing? Last night we all sat drinking Spanish wine.

Last time when Billie was here, if he really was here, we had French wine. He sat near the harp, he touched it with his fingers, and it lurched sideways; the flaps on either side of his driving cap, stupid cap, echoed the slightly closing mouth. Minute shiverings from the little glass things and the little china things, a thousand tiny dying vibrations in the crowded room.

'Well, I must be off ... I'll call tomorrow ... if I may?' A charming hesitant bending of the balding head, the knowing eyes quite sure, quite unmoved.

The following day we went to the pub next door and sat on high stools, and in spite of the years spent apart, and the millions of words written on paper and posted in boxes, we sat silent...

'I think of you constantly. If I said come out here to me, with the children, would you?

'I sat on the balcony overlooking the harbour, Sydney Harbour, and watched the lights and thought of you. I drove in the bush last night, the gum trees sprawl in the dust, we shot a kangaroo later. When it was skinned there was a naked flesh-less baby, not quite breathing. I thought of you.

'How you would revel in this heat, how it would suit your unconventional ideas of summer dress.'...

A memory of the few warm days in the back yard of Morpeth Street. A smudge of dirt on a stomach under sun oil, a line of black specks, a necklet of soot beads across a throat. There I lay imagining me beautiful and loved and unsullied, wholly unaware (O happy days) of just how pitiful, how callouse-footed, stringy-breasted, unbelievable I was. I did not then believe in heritage, in what is handed down—the curve of bone, the thickness of the skin, the placing of the limbs—I

33

thought all juxtaposed by brain and mind and lovely thoughts, enough to make a thing of glory out of nothing. And you, little Billie, dear heart in your funny hat, told me the truth. Which is not true, not true, It is not true. We went that last morning, after the drinks in the pub, the silent drinks, in separate cars, to Julia's home for lunch. I had to talk it out, I had to tell him something, he must help me to rebuild the image of myself he so cruelly broke (shattered, a knife thrust into the personality can lead to loss of life). Being deaf to my heart Billie did not hear anything I did not say, but Claud put us in a room, a room of flowers and low tables, to tear each other to pieces, a glass at each elbow. Why doesn't Claud come into the garden now? I need to see him.

'She's a sick girl,' Claud told Billie, shutting the door behind him. I had washed my hair, I really had, but it fell in strings on to my shoulders, and all that beauty I am so fond of talking about could hardly minimise two years of neglected sleep and nourishment. A naked face is more obscene than other things, the eyes burn without shade.

'I can't help it if I don't love you' (shut up, shut up), 'can I?'

The reasonableness of the charming voice was something not to be denied.

'I have been so ashamed of you, so embarrassed.'

Quickly, quickly, before all the air is let out of the sagging tyre, before we get to the iron rim, tell him, tell him.... 'But I've been ill, I have beeen ill. It was my father dying and the business with Joseph, and the baby....'

Aaah, we are down and out and flat and nothing more to hurt. Moving heavily from little table to little table, fingering the naval sword above the fireplace, Billie my Wild Colonial Boy extricated himself painfully from his dilemma.

'It wouldn't work, you must see that, you would never fit in with my parents.'

Dear God, a kick in the face, a removal of front teeth would be preferable to this. Summon enough air to say the words which are not after all true, but will help to stop the blood flowing quite so quickly.... 'I suppose really' (did I say it?) 'I never really loved you.'

The big boy spins round, an echo of all the other imaginary woundings, the old, for one instant, lovely sentimental Billie, the blue orbs fill slowly and clear immediately. . . . 'But I loved you.'

Silence. Love's last word is spoken, *chérie*. Such an emptiness, such arid desert in the heart. We can lose actualities, but to have dreams torn from us is too much.

The old funny car, the one Billie and I had loved in, went out of the yard. Claud and Lionel tapped the bonnet smiling. The round face at the wheel seemed so cheerful . . . a big wave, a touch to the cap on the head, a thin trail of exhaust rising in the warm air. Nothing more to do but hunch the shoulders and bow low to protect the damaged heart. Except to go for a walk with Claud along the road and cry out at each tree, because there was no one around to hear, and an arm round my shoulders (already not drooping quite so much) and a little chill breeze making us walk faster and faster. And the problem of what to do nowhere near resolved, as it is now, quite satisfactorily and with some sort of excitement. When Billie had gone Julia's mother made tea and Lionel, Julia's father, pressed me to feel his muscles, the tight little globes in the shrunken arms.

'Very strong, you know, my dear,' he said earnestly, looking into my pain-filled eyes, closing my fingers together whilst he flexed his wrists.

'It's just stormy weather, sail out of it soon, my dear.'

'Absent and sea-faring friends,' said my father every Christmas, raising his glass reverently and taking a quick look round to note the suddenly solemn faces. . . . 'God bless them.'

I hadn't any sea-faring friends then, absent or otherwise. I haven't now. Except Lionel, who is retired anyway. With what delicacy he talked, over the bread and butter, of islands he had known and dances he had danced, garlands round his neck, the skin on his face ('Here my dear,' feel') permanently roughened by harmattan winds blowing from Africa right up, right up (my fingers were slid up now to underneath the baffled eyes) to the upper New Guinea coast. Hot, dry, unbelievable.

The mind boggles, as Victorian Norman would say, sitting in the kitchen with the gas cooker lit for warmth.

How many nights sitting there, two years of nights, though I did go out sometimes. To the pictures, to the club, once to a matinée with Shebah, when she got hysterics in the interval, because she imagined the play directed at her, an accusation.

'Suspect goodness above all things,' she muttered. Wild laughter eddied from behind the locked toilet door; a woman applying lipstick half turned, a smear of scarlet appearing on her chin.

Other evenings, before Billie left, a fire in the grate, a candle on the piano, the pa pa pa of a ping-pong ball on the wooden floor. A kiss for the winner, a kiss for the loser, a burying of faces on the sofa, a reaching out for compassion. No callers, no knocks sounding from the brass knocker; once a visit from Claud beginning in the afternoon, and Mrs Ryan standing at the nursery window waving his car on, past the house, Billie's bowler hat on her head. The net curtain agitated, 'Later, not now sir, call back later.'

Surely then there was love. Impossible to remember.

Edward saw a bowler hat in the shop last night. His hand half reached up and fell again. The excitement of a bowler hat, the rakish delight it can evoke. Billie wore his bowler when he came to call when Joseph was sick in bed with one of his thrice-yearly illnesses, three days of reading, because he never had time normally, eating meals off a tray, a red muffler round his neck! 'How kind, how very kind'—eyes still on the page of his book, reaching out for the orchid Billie held, the friend come to pay a call, an excuse for us to whisper in the hall, to wrap arms about each other. Tonight, tonight, the strained waistcoat of the city suit—there's a button missing—a hand kneading my buttocks ('Up to the buttocks in mud they were, the cricketers of Flanders') a merry shout to the invalid upstairs, past caring, and the fingers reaching up to the row of pegs for the black and dashing bowler.

All this sun makes me dizzy. All this lying about in the grass among the daisies. One of the dogs has begun to bark, the one Claud says is feminine, the brown one, not the white one. Feminine for what reason?

'Be more feminine, don't scowl,' said Billie a year ago, speaking truthfully with the drink.

We sat with our backs to a wall, with a beach behind, sheltered from the cold. I wasn't brown at all. I wasn't really wind-blown, just a mess, with a rim of sand around my mouth. I resented our being there when we had so little time, when we could not return the hospitality (all lies, I was just so ugly), when all the women in the straggling garden were so well dressed in their casual clothes, and the right kind of sandals.

'Yes, I was there actually, at the time of the earthquake, were you?' The man in the denim shirt inclined his glass, not looking at me.

Billie bent his balding head in mock apology.

'No, I wasn't actually. Do tell me about it' ... and so on and so on until ... 'She's a television actress, aren't you?' His elbow, too sharp, dug into my ribs.

'No, I've walked on twice in *Biggles*.'

But it hardly mattered because the man was already turning away to have his glass refilled. Billie and I walked back in silence to the hotel. Not quite sober he pushed me heavily into the white bedcover. 'I won't, I won't,' my voice low in case they heard me in the next room.

'This is the first time you've ever resisted me.'

'You're a snob. You have to keep trying to impress people.'

'I can't help it if I like meeting people. It's not snobbishness to talk to people who have boats and holiday villas.'

'Why can't we get married?'

'I couldn't do it. If you knew the number of times I've arrived from London, tired and hungry, to a badly cooked meal in that sordid house ...'

Tears dissolving pictures of long preparations for dream meals, the money taken from the gas meter to buy salad and bottled beer. It's not fair ... I tried. I did try. Weakly the body abandons itself to a love act in name only; ham with its edges curling stares upwards from a cracked plate. Grains of sand, leaving my hair, slide down the starched surface of the white pillow. The faces in the hotel dining room of an evening turned to catch words murmured over the limp curves of melon. No need to worry about the hotel proprietress, understanding perfectly why Joseph, having brought us all to the seaside, could not be accommodated in the same hotel.

'I may have a friend coming tomorrow,' I tell her. Already the Wild Colonial Boy is thumbing a lift across the counties, bowler hat in carrier bag along with the soiled pyjamas.

'Among the dropped linen, the chemical apparatus,' said Shebah (something learnt in the days when she could see to read), 'there is a kind of loving.'

'Will you have a room for my friend?' Head down I stumble through my explanation. 'My husband is leaving tonight, though he will come back for us at the end of the week.'

The hotel-keeper whirls her cake mixture round and round the bowl. There is a room. Soothingly the spoon goes round, smoothing away lumps, creaming into perfection.

'Make the most of what time you have,' she tells me, 'never waste time.' She is not talking about my holiday, incredibly, this woman with the unremarkable face and the nothing remarkable figure. But then there is a husband in the outer parlour, clothed in a dressing gown, constantly drinking, allowed at last to devote his time to it, without fear of breaking yet another promise. 'It hardly matters now,' she confides, 'it being no longer of any importance what he does.'


Four days on a windy beach, a drink of coffee in a shop at night, some drinks in a garden. 'I can't, after all, marry you,' and up the road goes my love with thirty shillings of mine and the bowler on his head, and Joseph coming round the corner in a hired car, and me changing my despairing departing wave to the figure shambling up the highway, to one of greeting, with fixed smile and ... 'Here comes Daddy, children.'

If only I could understand, though Victorian Norman and I between us have analysed it with precision, so I should understand why it hurts, being loved, not being loved.

A sharp burst of laughter is needed this moment on the grass.

Of course the children don't suffer, have not suffered. Do banisters smile? Do we cows go to sleep in chairs? Last night it was Edward who went upstairs twice, away from the smoke-laden kitchen, to see if they slept peacefully, were covered by the blankets, were safe in their bunk beds.

Billie said that last day, in the room with all the low tables... set by Claud ... 'You neglected them dreadfully. I shall always be ashamed that I participated in their neglect.'

Was it neglect when I spooned egg into my girl baby's eye? The moist, tiny morello lip (dark with Ribena) quivering, the eye blinking, the freshet of crying. Or the sheets, not quite clean in the painted cot?


On the morning of March 26th Billie woke Colonial brown under striped sheets and said he would go to an hotel for a shower. The big boy, who had lived in a room full of leaves (the window would not close) with a dozen bags of old and rotting socks, a mound of clothes, stained and used to clean the car, fingers of nicotine and toenails far too long, half leaning on an elbow and looking with distaste or detachment at the grown children, desiring to have a bath before nine in the morning. Right, let him go to an hotel, don't mention the dream of getting on a bus together to take Boy to school, my clean blouse, my cleaned shoes; how my hair would shine if he chose to look.

June 9th, in Claud's kitchen, fifteen minutes to Edward's birthday, let us celebrate. Victorian Norman laughs wildly, the yet uninjured Shebah, eating with gulosity, rocks in a spasm of delight.

'Ah, darling, a birthday, happy birthday to you, happy . . .'

'Not yet, wait, it's not time yet.' Claud, only half convinced he is having a good time, brightens at the thought of more hours of words and verbal torment. Of us all, he alone knows why we talk so much, of us all he is the one to meditate with. On the telephone we called our partners by their initials. S, for Sally, gone with the children, never to return, and J for Joseph. Now J and S we said (like a chain store, buy your underclothes at J and S) should really have married. Same types, an element of detachment, able to be cool and put aside emotion.

'All right, all right, so some girl opened her legs to me, but do we have to be so intense?'

'Oh, please don't talk like that, it's love you're taking to pieces.'

'Keep your voice down. Let's be civilised.'

'Living with you is like standing on guipure lace. It looks like beauty, but it's full of holes.'

'Oh, very poetic. I'm going out for a walk.'

Under the table on my right Edward presses my knee; Victorian Norman on the left pushes my shoe with his own. Our eyes do not meet, only Claud looks at me, he mouths without a sound, I love you, I love you. Only Shebah sees, and lets her mouth grow petulant. Any admiration or attention should be directed at her.

Edward has been so good this weekend about the children; shielding them from the dogs, from being afraid.

Billie tried to be nice to the children but they were very young. He did take them to the Park, packet of bread apiece to feed the ducks. Two ducks on a pond, a blue sky beyond, something and something to remember with tears. That very first contrived meeting ... an afternoon in winter, baby girl in her pram, a pink outfit, the woolly hat on the bald pale head, fontanelle palpitating, small particles of soot at the corners of the closed infant eyes. 'Hallo,' the bowler hat is lifted not quite comfortably, the black shoes splay out as he walks. 'She's very white,' looking down at the sleeping baby.

Was that the moment that he knew it was impossible, in spite of falling in love, because the child was so small and the pram so grubby?

'I think you're wonderful....' Boyishness oozes from him.

I had never known a man who went into pubs, who smelt of beer, who smoked tobacco, who went to football matches, who drove a car and had men friends.

Concerts I went to, until I whistled too loudly once and Joseph said I didn't really like music, and evenings with red and white wine in a circle with nobody speaking a word of English and no one bearing a name you could possibly pronounce. And exhibition openings, and walks round the docks in the early evening, twined together, Joseph with his arm about my slender pre-marital waist, eyes moony with love reflecting the early moon above and the little lights strung out like beads across the river, and staring down at the rusted decks of the foreign boats sitting squatly in the oily water, with ropes like snakes curled in mounds and a cat licking its paws, and everything, because of the moon and the lights and the love, flaming and shining with points of brilliance. And then the dinners for six or seven, wine with each course and ... 'Well, you see painting doesn't purely represent the visual aspect' ... and ... 'I thought Bernard played a little too fast' ... and ... 'Maybe I should take up philosophy.' Of course we must lead beautiful lives, only I thought that was what we were doing, and quick put out the light before the positions assumed become too ugly. I did like music. I had a boil once on my face that swelled and swelled and would not come to a conclusion until one night at the Philharmonic they played a great loud thundery piece of music and a man at the back with a waxed moustache stood up and held wide his arms and clashed his cymbals together whilst my boil split open and spilled slowly down the side of my nose.

Billie and I went dancing. Oh, I love you, I love you, the

jigging up and down to the steel band.

'Let's meet somewhere away from here for a drink, if you can get out. The Railway Hotel, Widnes.'

A beer, a whisky and two pieces of pie, six men in the bar, papers out, smoking cigarettes, an octuple of wet lips sucking at glass rims.

'Let's sit in the car by the canal.'

Let us do that for God's sake. An impossible car, huge and conspicuous and splendid with leather seats cold from the rain drifting down. Darkness, a faint spattering of rain on the bowler hat, ploplets in the canal as rats moved, hands fumbling on impossibly thick suitings. 'Please touch me . . . please.'

A nonsense of threshing bodies, grunts stifled, the bitter taste of beer on his tongue, and a dozen small boys swarming and squealing about the bonnet. And more dancing and more evenings in the kitchen, and then the other public houses, the one in China Town with the paper lanterns with the little figures going round and round and the landlady, vast bosom enclaved in papal mauve, smiling, nodding the face under the purple hat so that the feathers waved and trembled pianissimo, and me on a stool aware of my face in the mirror behind the bar, a parched mouth painted red, two eyes, a lot of hair hanging around my neck. On the stool Billie's thighs splay out, he pats himself tenderly to make sure the buttons are secure. . . .

'Go on, another whisky.'

'Why do we always go to places with lots of people? Why can't we be on our own?' The drinking is making me aggressive, making me say things I mean.

'I thought you liked being out. I thought you wanted to come here. I could do with something to eat . . .' mildly the blue eyes try to catch the barmaid's attention, the feet stand square on the floor. The man's stance, a firm hand reaches into the back pocket of his trousers, the jacket rides up above the hips, on the top of the balding head hydrosis beads form and glisten under the lanterns.

'Oh God, you always think of your stomach.'

The body turns, an arm jerks me clear of the stool, my feet in their heeled shoes twist on the lino. Home, the dark hall in the dark house, the kitchen door opening, Brenny the baby-sitter calls . . . 'Everything's all right.' The door into the living room is ajar, it remains so throughout. It is not yet nine o'clock.

'It's not always my bloody stomach. It's not. It's not.'

The springs of the worn sofa sag, my spiked shoes catch in the fabric. I cannot breathe. Without removal of clothes, without pause for words, without the chemical apparatus, orgasmistic love occurs, begins, continues, for a year, for two years, everlasting, perdurable, God only wise. Not quite everlasting.

Claud sent me three drawings to hang above the brass bed. Tacked up with red drawing pins the Black Brunswick departs; tears trickle down the cheeks, percolate into the cavities of the ear ... 'I'll send for you. You'll see, I'll find myself ...'

'Your hundred best tunes' on the wireless, a last lingering look, the door with the brass knocker closes behind the Wild Colonial Boy. Years begin to pass in months and days. Not a week goes by without a letter from the Black Brunswick, now at the front, whisky bottle by his side, moths circling around a balcony overlooking the Tasman Sea. An insect, something hot, nipped then at my wrist lying against the grass. Shall I give a mew of pain, for protection, to break this silence and let Edward touch my hair?

Everything had turned out so well, so much better than desired. Last night the sentences flung across the shepherd's pie. . . .

'Oh, you're terrible, darling, you're no fool, you always get what you bloody well want, and so innocent with it.'

'I reckon we never get what we want, or only the half of it.'

'I think it's a bloody marvellous life.' Three pairs of eyes turn to Victorian Norman. Julia and Edward drink more wine. What are they thinking behind the bland expressions? We also serve who only stand and wait.

'You mean that?' Claud is merely leading Norman on, waiting for him to become entangled.

'Yes.' Emphatically the grape-intoxicated mountaineer thumps the table. 'Yes I do. I live, I copulate' (a snort, an animal noise of contempt from the nun with the bangles), 'we had a bloody wonderful time in Morpeth Street. Good friends, damn fine evenings round the table, eh?' The nostrils flare as the laugh billows out, an arm, roughly, to hide its sincerity, crooks my head and shakes me like a dandelion.

'I reckon,' says Claud, 'you're right. I reckon that Edward here should cleave to this woman. More wallop, man?' He shakes the victor's shoulders.

'No, no more.' Edward is thinking of later, and so is Claud.

'I should have brought my hat ...' I loll weakly against Edward, (pretending), so that he will feel I belong to him. The little girl with the innocent eyes, bewildered (I've had so much unhappiness) begins to tell the story, making herself so lovable. Apart from Shebah they do find me lovable.

'I've had that hat for years, a wedding hat, not actually that really but a *chapeau de la* wedding, and I've always worn it on certain occasions. I wore it when I fed the children in the night and when that policeman was calling and chained his bike to the railings, and when we all went to the club, and that night Claud came and he wore that Indian frock coat that somebody left behind. ...'

A trill of loosed laughter from Claud. 'Ah, that little blonde going with me to the chippie for those Chinese roll things, with all the little bits inside ... such a dear sweet thing. She thought I was a priest.'

Victorian Norman spatters his remembrance, the nostrils curve backwards. He remembers the blonde with delight.

'Do you remember, she got attacked the night of my father's funeral ...' I begin to tell about it but trail off, because of Edward. Should one joke about a funeral, about my Papa, my little plantation weed with the cheekbones and the stained homburg hat?

'Yes, you told me.' Claud does not know but he understands my dilemma, his head wags and a globule of red wine shakes from his gold beard and stains the cloth. His eyes wrinkle at the corners with tenderness, the moist mouth is wiped, I have to look away. Julia puts the kettle on, a wing of dark brown hair falls across a smooth, smooth cheek (the saviour of the world, she saved Claud's life, I owe her my sanity), lights the gas.

I did wear my hat the night they buried Father, the night they attacked Lizzie, the little blonde and giggling Lizzie, in the foggy street. All morning I travelled on the train to reach the church, and it took two trains to get there, because one could get no further in the fog, and I and others (several women, two little girls, a man with a cough) sat in a waiting room for a long time three miles from the village. Minutes ticked by in the frozen room, no lipstick on so that I would look more grieved (ill, sad), more suitable. Little Dad, not possibly dead. The only night for months I had (intended) an early night. The sea of covers on the brass bed, a needle of insistent noise niggling the brain. Footsteps coming downstairs; I won't answer, sticky darkness, waves of sleep, and Norman standing by the bed and saying ... 'Flower, it's your mum. I think you had better talk to her.'

I know what it is but I pretend I don't as I pad up the hall. Last Sunday he didn't leave the car to see me and the children on to the train. That irritated me; I thought he ate too much and took too little exercise. When the train passed the crossing, the car was still there, the children pressed stubby fingers against the glass and waved to the old man bent over the wheel. I meant to ring him when I got home to see if he felt ill, but I never did.

'He's dying, Maggie ... he's dying.' The voice, doll-sized, twelve miles away, moaning in my ear...

'Now don't be silly, keep calm.'

And further off still, and yet clearer, another voice ... o my darling, o my darling, o my darling.

All the way to the house I just wondered what to do if he had died and I could not cry. And he had died and I did cry, only not for that. A phone rang ('You answer it, Maggie'—a kitchen of neighbours, but me the only relative, the next of kin) and the quiet surgical voice of the doctor. ...

'He never reached the hospital. He died in the ambulance.'

Mouths in the doorway, all open, black holes waiting to swallow the news.

'Oh, the poor man, the poor man.'

I hold my little mum and put her on the sofa; my hand still holding a cigarette spills ash on the white cover. In the midst of death be careful of that ash, and the tears starting, big ones, tired ones, noisy ones.

At the funeral the hearse kept vanishing in the fog whilst we followed slowly; we almost reached him but then he eluded us. At the church, four paid gentlemen in black took him away in his wooden box on their shoulders and bore him away into the mist, so that it was a double shock, bent in the pew, to straighten and see the coffin, oh such a little coffin, right alongside me, near the altar rails. White wood with one wreath of flowers on top, and underneath a cold blood relation. A lot of words about how cheerful he was and how he had always had a cheerful word (God forgive him for the years and years of never speaking) for everyone, not mentioning the fact that he suffered from severe melancholia at least once a month, nor mentioning the misery he caused my mother (the long evenings sitting in the bedroom with red eyes, the sugar bowl dented because it missed her and hit the wall behind, the smashed window in the hall—'The blitz, you know, surprising isn't it?') nor the nights he lay huddled in a blanket face to the wall, grey, bitterness tramelling deep grooves in his yellow face. My mother in the front pew cries tears, snuffles fan out the veil of her hat. The deaf man in the coffin, the child's coffin painted prettily nursery white, lies feet pointing at the vaulted roof. 'Don't cry, my pet, don't let him upset you, run out into the garden and play.' The four men swoop down easily to lift him up, fog rolls up the aisle, they walk towards the black hole at the mouth of the church, and feet shuffle after them. One luminous tear rolls on to my brother's nose and is wiped clear with his handkerchief. How slowly we move behind him, one foot after the other, following him, but not all the way, the procreator of my hooked nose, my calid eyes, my skeleton of bones; how dark it is, how sad it is, how high the curved roof. One foot after the other we track the vanishing body … going now my Lily of Laguna, out of the door, O he's my lily and my rose, gone, carried by four strangers towards a millennium of sleep.

'It was a bloody marvellous hat,' Victorian Norman said, wiping bread round his plate, head thrust forward on his thin neck. The way he looked at me he was not quite sure whether it was genuine grief over my father or the presence of Edward.

Claud somewhere in the house has put a record on the gramophone. Music covers the garden. It should soothe Shebah but of course it might incense her. She does not move. I cannot tell if her eyes are open or shut behind the dark glasses. Billie did not like her ever. She kept telling me she'd met him somewhere before, at a poetry group, at a drama meeting, something very unlikely. 'It's not possible,' I said, but when they had come face to face in the kitchen they had known each other, and he would not, could not say why he disliked her so, though it was probably that he knew she distrusted him, was not sufficiently dazzled by his charm, resented him being in the kitchen, because finally it would be her that would be led up the hall, talking volubly, stalling for time, leaning in mock or real exhaustion against the wall, festooned with parcels and carrier bags (her little bit of fish for tomorrow, her bottle of cooking oil, the carefully wrapped quarter of *wurst* in greaseproof paper, last Sunday's paper folded at the theatre criticisms) the belt of her third coat buckled at the middle. She who would be handed from step to railing, which she would clutch in a frenzy, other arm held out to balance her, a one-sided Christmas tree, the carrier bags hanging straight down; she who would be waved to as she ran stumbling along the gutter, the Black Nun of Morpeth Street (I never took the vow of silence) hearing the big door with the brass knocker close behind her, imagining me running full tilt up the hall and into the arms of Billie, our two laughs mingling, our faces touching. Which is what did happen.

Later, when Billie had gone away and become the Wild Colonial Boy, there were nights when she did not go, winter nights when beginning to run along the gutter buffeted by wind and rain, in black darkness I would call—'Shebah, stay, don't go'—and the little Hebrew figurine would pad back along the passage, detesting her dependence on me, for more talk, more stewed tea (you turn your back whilst I wash), the grey pigtail would be released, the boots removed, the two coats, one macintosh, two pairs of gloves hung up to dry, the bed made up for me on the sofa, the light extinguished for modesty (hers as much as mine) the groan as she hauled herself on to the high plateau of the brass bed, the wild squeal of laughter as she lay half in half out, the call to God for help, the cry of damnation on all her bloody relations, the wind rattling the shutters, a child in the adjoining room, coughing once, twice, at last ... 'Good night, darling' ... and silence in the room, one-in-the-morning silence. To be broken by Victorian Norman walking as if up a rock face, along the hall and into the kitchen for his clock, the muttered chat on the telephone with his automatic time exchange ... 'Thank you ... thank you very much' ... the sound of the clock being wound, the locking of the door, a wild explosive sound of rage from the brass bed, but nothing articulate, and then two sets of snoring, one loud a foot or so away from me, one faint, from the recumbent Norman, stark naked and arms flung wide on the truckle bed in the room above.

Victorian Norman knows a lot, understands a lot about me, about Claud, and about Edward and about himself. What about Julia? Did he really seduce Julia last night whilst Shebah was talking words with Claud? Maybe on the bus he will have time to tell me. Last night it was nearly Edward's birthday.

'Ah, darling'—Shebah sounded reproachful when told, as if it should have been her birthday. Edward looked embarrassed and lit another cigarette.

'We'll make a night of it,' said Claud, looking at me.

We stayed round the table and its dishes, beginning not to be so conscious of our separateness, prepared to imagine we were truly friends and comrades. Above Claud's head were nailed two little painted heads in china. Two lovers with ruddy cheeks, and hats on, temple to temple, mouths pouting as if to turn and kiss. The smoke curled up into the air. A lone car drove past the window, headlights caught the painted heads for an instant and froze them, made them ugly, cracks minutely appeared across the china faces, and then they fell back into the shadows, tender, gentle as before.

'If you don't mind,' said Edward pushing back his chair and standing upright, 'I'd like to spend the beginning of my birthday in bed.'

Not even Shebah laughed. We looked at him and I said: 'Of course,' and he said good night politely to them all and bent his head to go through the low door into the shop.

'I reckon,' said Claud, 'that one's all right.'

I sat for five minutes feeling womanly and important, and smiling at everything, and when I left them to go upstairs Victorian Norman was standing at the sink with his arm round Julia, and Shebah and Claud had their heads together in a parody of the rustic lovers.

Edward was in bed, leaning on one elbow, watching me come through the door.

'Happy birthday.'

'I love you, I love you,' he said.

'Here's your present. Change it if you don't like it.'

I laid the striped shirt upon the coverlet of the bed.

'It's just perfect.'

'Many happy returns.'

'I love you, Please I love you.'

I was worried in case whilst we kissed his lighted cigarette burnt the blankets.

'Let me go and do my teeth.'

I could hear them talking and Shebah shouting downstairs as I washed. I didn't know what to do. I kept remembering what Victorian Norman had said I must do, and I kept thinking I must do it, and yet I wished I could just tell the truth. There was an awful lot of hot water, but I felt Edward might be hurt if I took so much time washing, so I just rinsed my face and put some perfume of Julia's behind my ears, and some on my tummy, and combed my hair. Then I went and got into bed and Edward switched off the light. Once the light went out I felt as if I was wrapped in cotton wool and a million miles from anyone, and there were so many things going through my mind.

Edward touched my cheek gently. 'It's a lovely shirt. It really is a nice shirt. Thank you.'

My cheek on his shoulder, damp with heat, eyes wide staring into the darkness.

Billie said we'd have a house in the country eventually and we'd get a dog for the children. Did he think about what breed of dog for what number of children even whilst he enquired about going away, even while he worried about emigration papers and formalities?

My grandmother when asked how she felt used to say ... 'Very nicely now. I had my womb scraped and the doctor said I've been a good clean girl. Now that's something, isn't it?' ... at eighty-four the good clean girl smiled childlike into the enquirer's eyes.

'Is it really your collar size, Edward?'

His hand stroked my hair to cushion my disappointment.

'Well, not really, but it doesn't matter, really it doesn't.'

'We could frame it and put it on the mantelpiece.'

We laugh, he wraps huge arms about me, delighted at the image of our home, our mantelpiece. Silently he roamed over the floors of a dream house.

Not quite so lonely. I could almost tell him, only I know at the end it would leave me purged and reborn and anxious for physical contact and he would be withdrawn and miserable. And Victorian Norman said I must not tell him, not ever, if I wished this time to be peaceful.

'Why are you crying?' Edward touched my eyelids with his fingers.

They felt like paper and they smelt of tobacco and I said ...

'Because I'm happy.' Which was the truth. I cannot help my ephemeral emotions. I decided long ago it is my greatest weakness, this inability to sustain any sense of misery, a dreadful superficiality that is as much a part of me as my hooked nose and my large mouth, which I can do nothing about.

'So am I, you make me happy.'

The mouth closes on mine, eyes close, hearts beat faster. Outside the room a chorus begins. 'Happy birthday to you, happy birthday to you, happy birthday, dear Edward ...' There is a great deal of laughing, of shuffling, someone (Claud of course) begins to turn the handle of the door. I laugh loudly to let them know it's a great joke, spluttering my appreciation against the smooth breast of Edward who lies stiffly, and beneath the noise Julia says ... 'No, Claud ... no,' and they move away still singing, a little band of happy wanderers.

'They do mean it kindly,' I tell the silent Edward in the darkness. Though of course they don't, at least not Claud. Not unkindly either, just that they want to protect me, most of all from myself.

Heads on the pillow again, breathing into one another's faces, faintly I can hear Shebah singing alone. 'Let's start all over again, Let us be Sweethearts once more ...' When she has sung it enough times she'll stand up and dance to it. At the last two lines she'll gather up her short skirts in her hands, lift one plump shoulder and shout almost in tears ... 'Though the fault it was mine, To fogive is Divine' ... a long pause then a toss of the now youthful girlish head of thirty years ago, a coquettish flutter of eyelashes, and a sideways canter into imaginary wings ... 'So let's start all over again.'

How the Black Brunswick would have doted on that sentiment. Clasping his Emma to his military breast he pleads that she forgive him. On the wall above the brass bed the Black Brunswick's Return curls at one corner. The drawing pin has rolled under the carpet. He is so tall, so protective, so splendid. She is so forgiving, so winsome, so drooping.

The night before Billie did return Victorian Norman watched me try on some clothes.

'How did he used to like you?'

'Oh, sort of arty I think.'

Once I had a white coat like a smock and he said in the street, 'Oh, my little Rose of Sharon. O, my little pretty.' Maybe he didn't. He did sometimes say I looked nice.

I tried on a check shirt, dark, and a striped sweater. Victorian Norman shook his head above the starched collar.

'No, not really.'

A brown and black dress, very tight (split under one arm-pit) and too short (my legs are funny), a dark background for a naked face, eyes forgiving, a winsome expression. Norman likes it, he likes the split arm-piece and the frilled petticoat that hangs down.

'He'll think it a bit messy,' I say, and take it off. 'I've got to appear as if I've made an effort, but am really not superficial or made up, just the old eternal child of nature I ever was.'

Norman laughs and goes on reading his paper.

Nothing seems the thing to wear, my face looked empty in the blotched mirror over the sink, or maybe it is my face that is blotchy. I have two lines on my forehead, just above my nose, as if I have frowned for two years.

'What's the date?' I ask Norman, hidden behind the newspaper.

'March the 24th,' Norman says, reading from the newspaper.

Two years ago and two months. With tears and love and ... there are no words, only enormous dreadful emotions.

'Why didn't I go to bed early?' I ask Norman, looking at the dark circles under my eyes. 'Last time I attempted an early night was when Father began to die.'

Norman puts down his paper on the table and rises to his feet. There is a look in his eye that I clearly recognise. He even finds the dark circles under my eyes attractive.

'Shall I put a record on?' I ask him, and busy myself with the gramophone so as to avoid his attentions.

I put 'Party Doll' on and twisted my hips, but suddenly neither of us was convinced, because all the other nights when we made a noise and played the oldest records (why did they all have meaningful titles—'I'll never make the same mistake again', 'Sweetheart', 'Somewhere in France with you', 'Silver threads amongst the gold, dear') the mornings were propheciable and Tomorrow wasn't, and Norman may have been uneasy because he wanted me to be happy and we both knew it was going to be (disappointing, sad, not a miracle ... did we?) so I went to bed without washing properly and before I turned out the light I kissed the photographed face of Billie. And truly I did feel different. I did feel safe and happy and hopeful and almost innocent and I closed my eyes with the image of myself so wonderful, quite intact and perfect.

Edward said, out of the darkness ... 'I don't want this to be like anything else.'

Had he said something before that? A long pause.

'I want it to be permanent, Maggie.'

'I want it too. Only I want time.' I didn't really. I couldn't afford to want time.

'Why?' Calm, reasonable Edward, my bedfellow. 'Why do you want time?' A cavalcade of reasons, none of them the real ones, strung out across the dark pillows of the visitors' bed. On March 25th the Black Brunswick returned. At six the children went to bed, at six-thirty I was washed, combed, perfumed; a fire burnt in the grate beneath the Sicilian lions, the brass bed under the white cover spun golden in the firelight. At the blue table in the kitchen I arched my eyebrows and thought beautiful thoughts to make my face tender, and folded my hands together on the lap of the dark plaid skirt, watching the shadow of the lampshade twist round and back again above the blue oilcloth. New lino on the floor carried painfully all the way from the shop two days before, an outsized waxy roll of honour, black and white squares oily under the rain. New curtains on the windows, white ones, hemmed with blue cotton (though only showing now and then), closed against a back yard under soot, a frail mountain ash leafless between slabs of concrete, five cats on a high brick wall. On the balcony of the house next door (boat-deck) the husband throws washing-up water in a flood down the wooden steps, loses the bucket in a welter of noise and slams the door into the kitchen. Two chops in silver paper already garnished and rubbed with garlic, on the draining board, a pan of sliced potatoes under water, two packets of frozen vegetables, one yellow, one green, to give colour to the white plates painted with columbine. The most important thing, Shebah had told me only the day before, is the expression reflected and transferred from the eye at the first moment of meeting. Practise it, liquefy it, it must be understood. I am here magnificent with confidence, over half a globe none more beautiful than I. Aaaah ... across the blue table half begins a moan, the throat constricts the ululation of defeat, a fist (mine) pushed apart my lips and touches the edges of teeth. Who are you? Name, address, parentage, don't lie, be kind to me, be kind to me. Under the innocent gaze I'm old and tired as well. Pity me, pity me. A knock on cue shatters the house, throws echoes down the hall, through the keyhole I can spy the Wild Colonial Boy, a blurred outline behind the glass, raising an arm to smooth his evaporating hair. Cold air as the door opens, a voice the ear does not after all wish to recognise, a face the eye fails to memorise, only a coat, a check coat, clean, beautiful and alien, comes into the house.

'Why?' again asks Edward.

Beyond in the other room, among the china, Shebah is still singing. Slowly the white arms stretch, the bangles begin to slither, the penitent cries ... 'Though the fault it was mine...'

Was I to have known the sun would have made him brown, bleached the line of hair on the cheekbone, paled the nails that tipped the tanned fingers; the palms open and show cream as he hands me a package. 'Go on, open it, it's for you.' Inside the paper wrapping is a box, a small jewel box with velvet backing. To the accompaniment of suitable music from a dream film, shot close up to show the dewy eyes of a girl opening her very first engagement ring, mouth curved in a tender tremulous smile, someone, me, picked out the toffee laid so carefully inside, unwrapped the paper, and placed the sweet upon my thick and bosselated tongue. Like a consecrated wafer it stayed in my mouth, my lips would not close. The figure opposite me, my defrocked priest, tapers down under the beautiful coat to two legs in light grey cloth, and there are two shoes, slightly pointed, new, dazzling. To avoid this, this slab of light illuminating my two years of darkness and sloth, I turn to the meat robed in its silver paper and light the grill. I have been too long entombed, too long used to neglecting my teeth, I have not begun to remember when it was I forgot the body can be a mirror to the soul.

'And you have been here all this time' ... the question is rhetorical, the stranger's eyes (blue irises circle the black pupils) narrow to take in without compassion, the dirt, the line of grease above the cooker, a car half hidden under the chair with the snapped back and a seat of green velvet textured with dust, and rest at length, twin orbs of empty brilliance, on my dark clothes, my white face, my fingers stained with meat juice. With the grilling of the chops, the twisting of the red-fringed shade above the oilcloth on the table, subastral love flickers, struggles to evoke some past echo of wonder and delight, and begins wholly to be extinguished. Still I fight for something, some interglacial period of reprieve, cooking the food, eyes down to the spitting fat, not looking at my executioner, my pen-friend, my blue-eyed doxy in the beautiful coat.

'I left my cases at the station. I ought to be thinking about looking for a hotel.'

He cannot be serious. The striped sheets on the brass bed go straight down without a wrinkle, laundry fresh and pristine. I cannot answer, words lie locked in the cupboards of an ailing mind, I cannot even turn round, bilboes of disappointment shackle my feet to the chessboard floor. We stand in the room with the fire at last, only the fire is nearly out and I have not the heart to put more coal on, and he keeps looking at each picture, each article of furniture, the brass candlesticks on the mantelshelf, the brass samovar, the stuffed owl in its case in the alcove, and when I look too, nothing shines any more, nothing glitters, everything bears fingerprints of neglect, the filigree neck of the samovar is cracked, the dulled eyes of the dusty moose stare at the Sicilian lions under a thin coating of soot; the whole room is a monument to despair, girdled in memories that are no longer of importance.

'You look tired.' (I too am a ruin of a memory, submerged under dust. Feebly I shake myself and moths, paper thin, fly about the room.) Dumbly I prepare for the night. The face washed with soap, the skin rubbed with the red towel (turn round—don't look), just for a moment I imagine myself an object of desire, and with the exposure of rice-coloured skin and the donning of the pink nightgown, huge, voluminous and ridiculous, release my conceit. I find my face cream and sit at the table. I am of course trying to be natural, clean, a honeysuckle girl not afraid to show a naked face.

'Hold the mirror for me.'

What am I doing? With each circlet of grease I rub away one more layer of romantic love; fingers without sensitivity destroy, erase the thin protective membranes of desire, and I sit finally exposed with shining nose and oily mouth, suburban, masochistic, waiting to be hurt. I move towards the cupboard to put my jar away, parodying the other figures moving at night across his two years of travelling; brown shoulders emerging from white shifts, golden girls fresh from baths and showers raise slender arms to push away the damp bleached hair. At last it comes—'Your ankles are so thick.'

A statement of fact. An observation of truth. An opinion.

City white in a pink nightgown, padding with flat yellow feet across the lino-covered floor, I take my swollen ankles.

Edward sits up suddenly in bed, dislodging Billie Boy. He reaches across the crumpled bed searching for a reproachful cigarette. I touch him for reassurance, his own, above the ribs where the skin is pouched.

'You see,' I tell him, though the explanation is for me alone, 'I've never had a bathroom before, or a bedroom that wasn't a living room or a kitchen that didn't let in the rain.'

A sound of air contemptuously escaping from his pained lips.

'A somewhat materialistic attitude.' The end of his cigarette glows in the darkness. 'Besides, I can well afford to let you have a bath and a bedroom seeing you place such importance on living accommodation.'

'Baths are important. Having a wardrobe to hang clothes in is important. It's not materialistic. It's romantic.'

My lips finish forming words and close to kiss his shoulder. Had I had a bathroom, a bedroom, a wardrobe, wouldn't Billie have continued to love me?

Scurring away from Edward I carry my skirt, my shoes, my underclothes into the bedroom that is a living room and lay them on the piano, and get into the brass bed quickly, taking my thick ankles with me. One of my shoes falls on to the dusty keys of the piano and a slight clear note is struck.

'I'll come back first thing in the morning,' says Billie.

'Yes.'

Sword by his side, the Black Brunswick from his place above the bed stares down at my upturned face. His arms in their military coat encircle the slender clinging Emma.

'I'll be very tender,' says the Wild Colonial Boy, bending down to kiss me. Neither he nor I can understand what this may mean. In a welter of cloth, in a dazzle of check overcoat, with a convulsive roll that is very adroit, a penetration unpremeditated and untender takes place, and a curtain of tears covers my face and swings sideways into my hair.

'You did have a bathroom in Morpeth Street.' Edward sounds accusing. 'A big one.'

'But I couldn't use it. Victorian Norman says it was dangerous. The geyser leaked.'

Behind a wall of flame Victorian Norman calls for help. In

the bathroom he stands dripping on his tiny black satin underpants, sulphurous flames sear up the copper side of the antique geyser.

'It caught fire once, Edward, when Norman was in the bath. So we all used the sink in the kitchen after that.'

Edward does not reply. Maybe behind his eyes he is consumed with the image of a room in flames.

The morning after the Wild Colonial Boy returned he reared up in the bed, the whites of his eyes luminous against his brown skin. He is like some animal. The children come in for his inspection, they stand watching him passively, faces placid. Every hair has been shaped so that he will say how lovely, every thought and idea planted so that he may say how well I have cared, trained, fashioned them. The long legs, the soft moist eyes, are Joseph's, eyes of Boy, bewildered, are my own. They watch without emotion the figure covered with hair. He says nothing at all. On the bus alone with them, fiercely I scan the lovely ones, the gentle ones, flesh of my flesh, tears endlessly and painlessly flow from my eyes and obliterate the streets we pass. Heavy lidded I laugh walking back to the house because I feel I am such a comic figure, and not for a moment to be taken seriously. What happened to the day I had dreamed about, those long hours of winding exploration, fingers tracing lines of unknown experiences on faces wet with tremulous emotion? I stood alone and watched with pity and with panic the blond stranger facing his disenchantment and could only turn away because apart from the ugliness of my weeping willow countenance, I irritated and appalled him.

'Never mind,' said Edward, 'it's my birthday,' and he stubbed out his cigarette and I muttered 'Happy birthday' into his ear, kissing his face all over, until he buried me under love and I went willingly enough, knowing how important it was to the future, blotting out all thoughts of Billie, only hearing above the sound of our breathing Shebah in the outer room, still singing her song.

From a distance later I heard Norman laugh as he went into the bathroom and I lay crumpled and said into the darkness: 'I don't mind about those things, the bath and the wardrobe, I do love you.'

And he replied, sleep drowning on his pillow: 'Then it's all right, it's all right, love.'

I felt calm and almost peaceful and a bit clever, until I remembered again all those other things, and had to turn away from him lest I might have clung to him and spoilt everything. And what would I do then, poor thing, poor thing.

It was like looking at an aerial landscape, very silent, with a network of little roads and hedges and rivers, and trees bunched like fists and saddles of pines flung over hills, and small walls made of stone separating handkerchief fields, and everything little and geometrical and in each square little groups of people moving, parents and relations and Joseph, and Shebah and Victorian Norman, and Billie in a matchbox car, and alone near a river, the children and I, looking up with pebble eyes. It was so ordered and on such a graspable scale and size that I felt the pattern of my life was not so complicated after all. All I had to do was take the children, one by each hand, and step over into another field to find something equally of comfort and delight.

In the next room I could hear Shebah continuing her burletta and Claud raising his voice to say some word or other, and I moved very carefully out of one side of the visitors' bed, and stood listening to make sure Edward still slept. He was sleeping (how could he?) so I opened the door and shut it after me and went to the bathroom to comb my hair and see what my face looked like. Whilst I thought, Here I go, pink-striped nightgown, solid legs and bare feet, hair so naturally, so wonderfully straight, a fringe over one melancholy eye, all in the dark and lips moving to verbalise the description of myself, I put up a hand and pulled the light cord. There was me in the mirror opposite, round-shouldered, lank-haired, hooked nose endlessly coming out of the Jewish intelligent horse face, a disappointment as always, and in the corner Victorian Norman and Julia in an embrace. Norman's laugh billowed out and Julia moved her hands blindly across the wash basin, reaching for her glasses. Almost at once Claud came into the bathroom and one arm reached out and held me against his shirt front. He said, 'Nice time, dear one,' and smiled fondly whilst the blue eyes took in with care the smooth pink face of Julia, the mouth open showing small irregular white teeth, the two buttons undone at the neck of her cream blouse and the eyes with black pupils enlarged, blinking once more behind the restored glasses. He laughed then and buried his head into my neck and said very low, 'Good God, girl,' and I knew exactly what he meant and nothing was solved after all.

After a time one has to pretend that certain things matter in order to appear normal, and it is all so feeble. At least it seems so if you are one of them (Victorian Norman's expression) and he licked his fingers to rub away a splodge of toothpaste on the mirror, but Julia, being definitely not one of them, but trusting and good and unsullied by endless repetitions of endless situations, found it convincing and followed Claud worriedly as he moved out of the doorway with slightly bowed head. So I combed my hair and Victorian Norman went on rubbing out the stains on the glass and shrugging his shoulders up and down to compose himself, and I did not speak knowing how he hates immediate discussion and that his mind would be full of thoughts of what he would have done and what he might have done had he not been interrupted, and he started to whistle very shrilly the tune of 'Sussex-by-the-Sea' and look at his reflection, and then we went into the living room and he stroked my bottom just as we entered so that I leaped almost on top of Shebah who stood still singing, flamboyant braceleted arms stretched out to an invisible audience, near the gramophone. She stopped in the middle of a note, a high caressing note, and said, 'Oh, darling,' sadly, and with entreaty, as if it were my wedding night and I had turned up at the celebrations. Claud gave me a drink and a Woodbine and I sat with my feet curled up under my pink striped nightgown (I will never willingly show my ankles again, Billie dear) in the big velvet armchair, and Shebah hovered above me, a pale swollen moth, furry and threatening, with eyebrows rising and falling and eyes dilating, voice hushed and confidential: 'What's happened, darling? ... Are you all right, darling?' and behind her the lovely room glittered and spun in a coalescence of glass and silver and gold.

There we were all together (Julia was in the bedroom repairing her lipstick), graduates of the University of Life, three of us immoral, cynical and lost, and the fourth, the black, music-hall nun, mad for half a lifetime, giving off tenderness, emitting signals of sensitivity. Victorian Norman, the amateur mountaineer, tight calves curving beneath the light grey cloth of his trousers, head respectfully and deafly inclined, listened with his eyes to the moving mouth of Claud, a small pink hole opening and closing among the tendrils of the climbing beard, speaking articulately and no longer with feeling, about his departed wife. 'There was real glory, men,' he repeated, 'real glory,' and we smiled at each other across the room, a smile that was split and finally obliterated as Shebah moved between us and stood with heavy loving face above me, peering down at me in the lap of the velvet chair.

'It's no good, darling,' she said, 'you can't deceive me' ... (It's possible she is right) and the broody lower lip swung lower and the eyes, sticky as sweets, searched my expression for some sign of response, some explanation as to why I had left my bridal bed, and a fat consecrating hand came down with a shiver of bangles to see if my forehead was hot to the touch.

'I'm all right, Shedah. Edward fell asleep, and I thought I would like a cigarette.' I shook away the pressure of her hand and leaned my head against the amber fabric of the chair back and noticed, as I folded my hand on my knee, how silver tipped the nails of my fingers. With my ankles stowed away, clad only in candy-striped cotton, with such a hand upon my knee, I could be any one of the golden girls, untalked about, that the Wild Colonial Boy had known.

When Julia came back into the room with adjusted hair and fresh-painted mouth, we all blurred together, came out of focus. She was so clean, so decorous, without guile, she represented reality, normality, we became stuff that dreams are made of, shadows in an overcrowded room. Shebah stood with hand on hip and began to talk to Julia, glancing at me from time to time, the rubber mouth stretching and spitting out sounds, looking like a welfare worker disguised as a woman explaining to her second in command what the blanket situation was, and I was an evacuee (lately young) waiting to be billeted. It made me laugh, what I was thinking, and Claud looked away from Victorian Norman, and I gestured at Shebah, but he looked at my hands and I blinked quickly and moved my wrists about and wondered if he thought my nails beautiful too. I felt a bit tremulous and hysterical with all the drinking and smoking, so I shut my eyes tight, and there was the check coat coming through the door, and it was as if a hand, any hand, had suddenly caught hold of my heart, which was round and hot and rolling about just above my ribs like an orange waiting to be squeezed, so that I dug my teeth into my lip and said over and over into my brain ... 'Who are you, what's your name, don't lie, what's the full name?' ... and the typed particulars stuttered out across the red birth certificate like a train going full tilt with swaying carriages, until gradually the squeezing stopped and little by little the heart filled out again, no longer in distress, only bruised. It wasn't exactly unpleasant, there was a kind of masochistic elation that I wanted to share, so I opened my eyes letting them be pain-filled, but neither Claud nor Victorian Norman was in the room to be appreciative, and Shebah, who anyway only responds when grief is evidently secretive, had her back to me.

I watched my fingers for a little, and then got up and went down the wooden stairs, under the flying angel at prayer and through the shop in darkness into the back yard scented with leaves and grass, sprinkled with maimed statues floodlit by the room upstairs. It was too cold to go very far; anyway I wanted to be noticed sitting at a wrought-iron table at night. I'm useless when I'm not noticed. I only really exist through other people (Joseph's opinion, pontification through the plum-soft lips), only start to breathe when mirrored in another's eyes. And why not? But something is altered, something is not quite right. It was lovely (decorative) in the garden last night, the day and the night I was circled by friends; there is a feeling, however, of strain at the roof of my mouth, as if I have started to yawn but forgotten to complete it. My mind never seemed to have spaces but more and more there is space, and the only thought I really have is visual, the check coat, and in the garden last night, seated at the iron table, when I looked at the wistaria tree with its twisted stem clinging to the centre wall of the house, leaves shifted, and there was the coat again, made out of fingers of light, black and white, with three round moving buttons. I cannot really see the coat if I actually try to imagine it, but it's always there when I don't expect it. I cannot see it now lying here on the grass, because I'm watching an ant nobbling under a pinpoint of soil, and perhaps given time, as Victorian Norman tells me, the picture will vanish altogether. The coat isn't a noun, it's almost a verb, it's I coat and You coat, though it's difficult to explain, most of all to myself, but fortunately I am by nature so transient, so superficial, that in time I'll stop thinking about it. I might have been a coat that opened and sheltered us both. I could have lain warm within it, just as the kitchen could have witnessed small fluting kisses and smothered words, a beating of hearts, a cautious exploration of emotions not entirely innocent. But he was so hostile standing in the cloth coat, wrapped up in it, hands in his pockets, in the middle of the kitchen.

In the morning we had gone a ride up an escalator past a garden party of hats, straw made and garlanded with flowers, like wedding hats, and there was a long mirror across the whole of one wall so that there were two rows of roses trembling on two rows of steel stems, and two check coats, and two checked arms resting on the moving rail, and two of me, with sulky face, love locked out, wearing my grief like a pair of blinkers over puffy eyes, resentful as we slid upwards to the roof of the store. I cried in little pieces all day, turning to get a knife from the drawer, bending to pull up the covers of the sacrificial bed; when I filled the sink with water the muscles of my eyes contracted and tears spilled out, and inside I began to slide away and saw everything all around me, the lino (just for you), the curtains (just for you), dissolving like bubbles in a glass. I didn't see Billie's face at all, because by now it wasn't a face I knew, and his voice said ... 'Hurry up, the taxi will be here in a moment,' whilst I just went on touching the plant in its pot, and touching the table, and Brenny made tea and nobody said another word.

In the taxi I sat far away and didn't mean to say it but did say it: 'When are you going?'

'I'll go tonight.'

A silence for years.

'Well, you don't really love me. ...'

'Yes I do, you know I do.'

A coward's reply. And the taxi stopped and while the check coat turned to pay the fare, repeating some action well learnt in childhood and unchecked, the sulky woman moved and ducked and ran down the lighted street full of buses and cars all in procession, and when I returned to the house later, much later, but not so late, he'd been and he'd gone, and Brenny and Norman sat stricken and the turtle's back had gone out of the hall, and the boxing gloves from their nail in the nursery, and the brass horn from the piano top, and I never saw him at the house again. Victorian Norman did. He came for some pictures and to say I had deteriorated physically (poising a cup of tea on the blue oilcloth) and I did use to wear my hair up to show my shell-like ears, oh yes, and then they shook hands and he went down the hall (a pity, a hell of a nice bloke) as he had done so many times before, only this time I was not there to put from behind my two arms about his shambling waist, and out he went, never no more, no more, no more ever to return, positively a last appearance, if indeed it was he who had returned in the first place, leaving behind nothing, nothing beyond the new lino in the kitchen and the new curtains turning already a rich grey and the top drawer of the chest in the hall stuffed full of letters in air-mail envelopes. If he had known (how could he?) as he went down the steps carrying his pictures, the landscape and the stags at bay, bending the pale flat tips of his stubby fingers to grip them more fiercely as they flared outwards in the sudden rain-filled gusts of wind, what he had left behind, would he have paused, borrowed a pencil perhaps and written some consoling words and thrust them through the brass mouth of the magenta door, to be added to all the other words on all the other bits of paper?

Last night at the wrought-iron table, under the pink-striped nightgown I pushed my cello thighs against my rice-white stomach, not yet swollen, and like a cow lowing in deep grass, swung my bell head, the hair swishing about my shell-like lobes, my darling, my lamb, my baby blue Colonial Boy, till blood sang in my ears.

Then another sound, a continuation of sensation, a hushed exhaling, and through the moving strands of thin hair, Claud stripped to the waist, arms aloft, wielding a spray filled with insecticide above his unbloomed roses. Caressing the sounds voices make in gardens after midnight, lungs gently rising and falling under pale rinds of sky, a hissing as the pump moved up and down and ... 'I reckon the thing to do is submit' ... this to the arch submitter in the night attire, the peachy one, mushy to the core, crouched over a wrought-iron table.

'There's little else I can do.'

I do think it's my suburban loyalties and limitations that keep me from being utterly an enemy of the people, at least in spasms, like last night when the father in me stirred, an icon head of narrowness with raised Victorian eyebrows, watching a disinfestation of roses at past two in the morning. Of course it was wholly me sitting there, but the foundling thoughts of puberty (not possibly could I have sprung from those Lily of Laguna lions) had receded altogether to be replaced by inherited modes of thinking, and the eyes that saw the near-naked landscape gardener where his eyes, alien, askance, bed before eleven, complete decorum in dress; but it was I who said with lullaby lips ...

'Have I done the right thing, Claud?' Meaning the birthday boy Edward upstairs in the visitors' bed, asleep all alone, and Claud said ...

'Mmm. I reckon you have. He's all right that one.' He sent another cloud of spray into the night air before coming to rest on the wooden bench by my table. There we sat with one arm stretched out, his, and a hand circling my cold little foot, my meek little toe-nails, and a moth, feeble in a ray of light from the upper windows, fluttering cloth soft and obscene above our heads.

'It won't be great glory, my love,' he amended insanely, rubbing a porous fold of diaphragm above the barrel of his ribs, 'however, it will be a solution.' He raised glossy eyeballs to the windows above and informed ... 'Edward from bedroom to bog with averted eyes, for the second time.'

'I'll go up presently.'

'I should.'

His fingers lay motionless across my feet. I leant the hard bone of my jaw against my rounded knees and a musk smell, faint from the folds of pink nightgown, rose pleasantly to my nostrils, dilutions of excitement long since over. The hand at my foot moved upward, surmounting the obstacle of my clasped hands and began to stroke the surface of my head, through which thoughts hop like so many sheep over fences.

The kitchen table in Morpeth Street spread with blue oil-cloth, franked one dozen times by the ringed indentures of a dozen mugs of tea, and my head with the medusa strands of hair down in two folded suffocating arms, safe from harm, deaf among the bristly fronds of a moaning purple jumper, part of the homecoming trousseau. One large empty bottle of gin, purchased duty free at the bar of the homecoming ship, perched like a skittle close to my fragile scalp, pulsating under the dark brown, mid brown bunch of hair. A wish to sleep and with the desire, a craving for the extension of sleep, a deathly oblivion, a ceasing upon the midnight (mid-day) with no pain, a desire not to be fulfilled as a sound very like the buzzing of a fly trapped behind glass, issued from the telephone with its black cradle hard up against the door. A voice, alas, not his voice, repeating a name, my name, making an enquiry, persistent, till with boredom I drop the earpiece with a dull plastic thud precisely on a white square of lino, the third from the closed and paper-choked door, allowing myself at last to fall beast-like on all fours, and slid finally like a leaf with the toes of my winklepicker shoes curled up, cheek to cheek with the cool surface of the floor, one finger held up for silence in the small groove under my nose (the imprint of God's finger in the wet clay) and went with mouth clumsily ajar, first with a gentle soughing of air, then with a frantic galloping of hooves, into a long cave of dreamless sleep.

Somewhere in the midst of all these painful recollections I had risen from behind my wrought-iron table and gone back into the house, leaving Claud alone with his roses. On the stairs I met Victorian Norman and we embraced beneath the benediction of the praying angel, and in the middle of something between a laugh and a sob I raised my eyes and saw Edward at the head of the stairs, standing above us wrapped in a peacock dressing gown belonging to Julia, a long tassel hanging from his waist to the toes of his big white feet, and I went quickly towards him and through the living room, where Shebah sat owl-eyed and unseeing on the arm of the sofa, and into the visitors' bedroom, presently to be followed by Edward, who allowed himself to forgive me, and I fell asleep. I dreamt I was in the kitchen again at home, and there was the tiny shivering sounds of distant bells that Fred the mouse made, in his little cage on the window sill, going round and round on his metal wheel, treading his little golden rodent road to Samarkand.

In the morning, this morning, early, without benefit of sunshine, only pale, cold drawn light, I crept from the visitors' room to go to the children, lest they awoke and finding me not there came in search of me. I went all huddled through the dim living room and saw through my dishevelled hair the sleeping body of Victorian Norman, safe in the bosom of the deep, the sofa, face turned from me, and a dog, the feminine one with the white face, sharing his temporary bed. On the threshold of my other room I stepped over a scrap of orange scarf tossed from the dancing neck of my Liverpool Salome, and came down sharply with the yellow sole of my left foot on to something like glass that bit into my flesh.

When I awoke hours later, with the remembrance of two loving arms about my neck, my little daughter's arms, rosy and possessive though now absent, I heard rather than saw Shebah, only a few feet away from where I lay in the lower bunk, stretched out on a camp bed, the black circumference of her beret showing above the army blanket, grey pigtail sticking out like a skein of wool, and groaning softly. Whilst I heard the gentle moans I still experienced, as I do most mornings, the split-second delusion that everything is all right, that Joseph, no Billie, loves me, and then reality and there I lay, the girl wonder with a mouth sour with nicotine and tongue swollen, entering the second day of a weekend in the country. I began to write an imaginary bill in my head, on a piece of paper neatly ruled, something to send to Billie, an account rendered for suffering received, itemed one, two, three, but I couldn't think of suitable words. So instead I imagined him somewhere, a party, a pub, anywhere, loosened with drink, telling someone, anyone, how a part of him still loved me. I do, you know, he intones, raising mild blue eyes angelwise to a blue heaven for ever out of reach. Wherever you are, however many years hence, my lovely William, may your well-bred mouth droop in unutterable despair. Amen. I don't mean that, I don't. Whilst I had these thoughts for which I may not be forgiven, Shebah groaned louder, called upon her Hebrew god and articulated ... 'What shall I do?'

And I asked across the felt carpet ... 'What's up, my dove?' and she replied in desperate tones—'Oh, darling, the damage I've done,' and wailed again, this time weakly, and I lay trying to fathom it all out, only was interrupted by Claud entering bearing tea on a tray made of tin painted all over with flowers. He sat heavily on the side of my bed and took hold of my chin in his fingers and shook my face a little from side to side.

'What's the matter with Shebah?' I whispered, and he let go of my chin and bent to reach the tea and replied in that firm voice he uses when something is wrong but he intends to minimise it—'Oh, we had a little accident. Nothing too bad, my love. Tea, Shebah?' and he got up kindly and sat at the bottom of the camp bed and pushed at something approximate to the buttocks of the moaning Shebah, who heaved suddenly and tragically from beneath her army blanket, with a head of fire like John the Baptist, rolling eyes and all. Sobs shook the room. Through the savage gusts of breath I made out the words

... so sorry ... so valuable ... it's no use, darling ... nothing is of any use ... all life is a cheat ... the prizes given at the children's party ... and then the head ducked again and only the woolly tail of hair was exposed to view. Like a professional dancing partner Claud rose again and come over to me and sat down.

'We had just a little too much wine and a little too much starting all over again,' he said, absentmindedly stroking my shoulder. 'She fell into the glass cabinet by the fireplace and there was a little broken glass.'

'All those china things' ... my mouth stayed open. After all she was my friend, my liability.

'No, one or two things, and one was something I'd mended before anyway, so not to worry,' and he broke into a smile and the eyes crinkled at the corners and he kissed my forehead.

'How did it go, the birthday night?' The moist little tongue licked out a tendril of beard.

'All right. What about Julia?'

He shrugged. 'All right too.'

We fell silent, just looking at each other. The point about me and Claud is that having talked so much in the past we no longer need to say anything, because we know beforehand. We now merely make symbolic sounds and let out thoughts run on and round the mile or so of electrical circuit inside our knowing heads.

Shebah had stopped crying or moaning. One eye larger than life, with a fearful glint of mock repentance, blinked naked over the hem of the sheet.

I laughed and Claud shouted—'That's better, me dear, have a cup of tea'—and put the mug by her side and went out into the living room.

'Darling,' said Sheba, in a stage whisper that could be heard in the next room and the one beyond, 'it's dreadful, it's just dreadful.' She scuttled frantically in the welter of bedclothes. 'I tripped on the rug last night and fell against Claud's cabinet with all those beautiful pieces inside, and the glass broke and several things fell against each other and got chipped, and Julia said "O Christ" and you know how charming she is, and Claud never said a word, he just went on talking to Norman and I felt terrible. I tried to see what damage I'd done and Claud shouted across at me: "Leave it, Shebah," very fierce, and Julia was then quite nice to me and sat down, but I felt

65

like dying. I wish I'd never come.' Here she gave a loud laugh of hysteria and I said:

'Oh, it's all right, love, everything's insured,' and again she laughed, more her old self, and stuffed one hand into her ruined mouth to smother the hilarity that was shaking the bed.

I went into the living room to see just how bad the damage was, but apart from a star-shaped hole in the front of the cabinet and some small pieces of glass that lay in the pile of the carpet, there was nothing, so I went to see if Edward was awake. The hospitable tea-bearing Claud was there also, sitting sideways on the nuptial bed, holding Edward by one arm. For my benefit Claud said loudly ... 'Stick to her ... there's great glory' ... and Edward smiled a little uneasily and held the sheet against his vast unclothed shoulders with fingers stained brown with nicotine.

I said: 'Hallo, Edward,' and Claud went out with his tray, this time looking for Victorian Norman.

I told Edward about Shebah and he looked concerned and there was a little silence till he said: 'I love you,' as if that was the only thing he had to compete with against the breakages of the tipsy anti-semite, and all the duplicities of Claud and Norman and myself. Myself mostly. And I do love him, will do (all this loving), and when I was getting my clothes on he moved suddenly and touched my belly with his hand and smiled into my eyes, so that I nearly said something like, do you realise that I may very well be pregnant after last night's carry-on, only I couldn't say it because he looked so happy and so good, and when I looked at my stomach it was quite flat really, so I just finished dressing quickly because outside the sun was shining, and we went downstairs and through the shop and out into the back garden among the statues, and it was warm and apricot golden. Like now, only it was so much earlier and that much fresher, and we had, or so it appeared, the little garden of grass beyond the courtyard entirely to ourselves. We kissed in the open air beneath the trees; there was dew on the grass and in the grass tiny white-faced daisies, and a bird sang on two notes, one high, one low, and I knelt down and put my two arms around his knees, and then came three sounds, or rather four, one after the other, like this—

'Coooeee, darling' ... a hidden recovered Shebah spotting Edward among the branches.

A laugh from the flaring nostrils of Victorian Norman, somewhere on the right.

A gun shot, and following the bright ping of sound, maniacal laughter not without humour, and standing up on the instant I saw Claud at the open window of the living room, an air rifle tucked into his shoulder, sunlight spilling off the metal barrel, beard mingling with the wistaria leaves as he leaned far out, one eye screwed up.

A low moan from the grass a yard away from where we stood, and Shebah, a fallen black crow, lying with powdered cheeks crushing the daisies. No one moved. Then another shot and Victorian Norman with clean collar and well-shaven face coming over the grass at us quickly, hissing: 'Lie down, the bugger's gone mad,' and obediently we fell down into the grass, like the spokes of a wheel, heads all touching, breathing on each other, and Norman laughing with his lips drawn back over newly brushed teeth and sweat running down the side of his nose.

Then blessedly the voice of Julia saying mildly, impatiently—'But, Claud, they're all out there in the garden,' and Claud shouted innocently with just the right shade of concern:

'Nobody hit, eh, man?'

At which Edward jumped to his feet and shouted back loudly—'Yes, you've shot Shebah.'

Then I got up and ran to her. There was a long felt pause. The little invisible bird whistled sharply above the body of the stricken Israelite. She lay on her side, one Edwardian leg bent at the knee, the fingers of her right hand stretched starwise. A tiny breeze blew grey hair in strands across the bunched drooping face in the grass. I knelt unbelievingly and one eye snapped open and fixed me with a look of hatred. The early morning lips parted and she said ... 'The dirty rotten Jew-baiter' ... and quickly struggled to cover the exposed knee with her too tight skirt. When we got her upright and dusted the soil off her and poured the thimble of whisky that Claud brought, between her sullen lips, she was beginning to enjoy herself a little. The damage was after all superficial. A slug had merely hit one of the statues close to the fence and ricochetted without much force on to her ankle. It hadn't even lodged in the flesh, but struck and trickled into the grass. Julia put a bandage over the mark, on top of the stocking, and throughout Shebah grimaced and groaned and bit her drooping lip and cast comical glances at us all. We put her in an easy chair just outside the back door, under the wistaria, with a stool to prop her injured leg on, and a travelling rug wrapped round her, and the sun shone and she looked like a passenger on a veteran car rally, and laughed wildly with elation. I kissed her cheek and felt that after the china breakages she probably felt better for being shot at, less under an obligation to Claud. She ate a big lunch and Claud for his part seemed to give her the tastier bits off the ham, and it will give her something to remember, something concrete, personal, to add to her list of Jewish persecution.

Meanwhile we lie here waiting to go to the bus stop to make the return journey. I could find it in my heart to wish there was no return. As Victorian Norman says, the mind boggles. I could stretch out my hand towards Edward.

If there was anyone there.

'She looks an interesting sort of girl,' said Stanley after a time. To which Claud did not reply. He touched the white plates in the sink with his fingers and looked out into the yard, at the small garden beyond the barn where Maggie and the others had posed for the photograph.

'Hurry, Claud,' she had said, 'we don't want to miss that bus.'

Shebah surprisingly had not minded the camera, minded it less in fact than the isolated Edward who had deliberately chosen to ignore Maggie's hand reaching to hold his. Apart from the proximity of their fingers there was nothing to show that she had attempted to reach him. But for the snapshot there was no reason to suppose there had ever been a gathering on the grass. It was the same old problem. When he cared to close his eyes did that tree by the wall cease to exist? When he chose to forget entirely his wife, to let her fade into oblivion, did she in reality no longer breathe and live in the world? His world? He remembered, too, all the other snapshots he had taken, all the other images, all the arms about all the waists, and all the faces, the same face, her face smiling into the sunshine, lips curved, with his arm about her so that they looked as if they were together.

'She's always in some sort of trouble,' said Julia, 'but she has amazing resilience.' She stacked the empty cups on the draining board and put away the sugar and the biscuits. She added not quite sincerely—'I have the greatest admiration for her.'

'What exactly is the trouble?' Stanley touched with his fingers the cheeks of the sweethearts glued to the wall. For the moment he had forgotten that he wanted to get away in his car with his wife and drive to his home.

'Well, it's a bit difficult really to say,' said Julia and proceeded to attempt to say it. . . . 'She had an unhappy marriage and then she met a man called Billie and then she got pregnant.'

Stanley said—'Oh, that sort of trouble'—and saw his wife was looking at him.

'Is Billie in the photograph?' she asked.

'No. No, he went away before he knew Maggie was pregnant. He went away once before to Australia but he came back again. But then she met someone else and they were going to get married, at least they were when the photograph was taken, only he went away too, and then she found she wasn't pregnant after all.'

'How convenient.' For some reason Betty was angry about the unknown woman who hadn't been pregnant after all. And she wasn't by nature uncharitable, she told herself.

'So she's all right,' she added, listening to the bitterness in her own voice.

'Maggie will never be all right,' said Claud.

'Oh.' Julia looked at his back, at his two elbows moving as he soaped his china in the sink.

'Do you really know, darling, or do you mean it's inevitable?'

Betty was startled at the use of the word, of that particular word, coming from someone like Julia. It did not seem reasonable that Julia should talk in the same complex way as the bearded man who had put his arm round her shoulders. She supposed that people living together must influence each other, though she did not feel influenced in the slightest by Stanley. But then they never talked about anything complicated. But that wasn't quite right. Neither Claud nor Julia was discussing anything very complicated, it was just that they managed to make things appear so.

She frowned and said before Claud could reply ... 'I do think there's a lot of immorality these days' ... and floundered, regretting something—'I mean an awful lot of people just put up with things. They don't give in.' And found Stanley looking at her face, as if she had betrayed them, as if she meant they were merely putting up with each other.

'There aren't any people who put up with things,' said Claud. 'There are only people who have neither the opportunity nor the need.' When he turned from the sink with soapy arms he was smiling. He was no longer aggressive. 'If you have ever been in the position of either Maggie or myself,' he went on, drying his hands on the same cloth with which he had dried Betty's foot, 'you can hardly know whether giving in applies. In fact it's just the opposite. Those who put up with it give in, those who cannot put up with it, cannot give in.'

'Oh, come now,' said Stanley, feeling liberated by the sudden friendliness apparent in Claud, in spite of his words, 'you must admit there's an awful lot of letting go these days.'

'There's not enough,' said Claud quite cheerfully, and took the photograph from Julia. 'Mind you, we let go a bit that weekend, didn't we, girl?' He put an arm round Julia's waist and she smiled up at him. She relaxed against him as if in confirmation of the fact that upstairs, stomach full of mother-lovely milk, the baby slept, flesh of their flesh, petal lips shaped against its cot sheet in much the same fashion as her own mouth lying crumpled against the front of Claud's shirt.

'It was a nice weekend,' she said.

She looked down at the snapshot into the face of Victorian Norman. 'You might have shown it me before,' she said mildly, 'I didn't even know you'd had it developed.'

But Claud had gone out of the kitchen and was in the front room of the shop attempting to clear a place for the newly bought plates. It was a pity, he thought, that there was not time to get to know everyone. That woman Betty, so smart in her costume with her pretty legs and her poor little unkissed breasts. And that unkissing husband Stanley, hopelessly normal and quite unable to communicate. Maggie would say that no one was normal, that in everyone abnormality was dormant, waiting to be released. He was not so sure. His wife had been normal, his lovely and his lost wife with the rounded arms that had never tried to encircle him, and the detached cool mind, terrible and vistaless as the floor of a glacier, upon which he had rolled and slid helpless as an infant. Victorian Norman was normal too. An army of strong and superior people marched through his head brandishing their normality like swords. If he could only rationalise why it was she had never loved him, it would not matter. It was the fault of her relationship with her father, the fault of her mother for letting her cry at birth ... the fault lay with her, with others, the fault was that she had never loved him. And it was not in him to be humble enough to accept that he was not lovable. Or that he was not normal. Everyone said that given time he would heal. Everyone said that Time was the great helper. If he wanted to be healed or helped then he would not now regard Time as an enemy. This was precisely the paradox. Time had given him his great love, his not to be stolen love, in Summer Time by the river, among leaf shadows. In Time he had walked with her and talked with her and slept with her, and soon Time would come and take away his memories and his recallings, removing them far off so that he could no longer see them clearly.

He could not find a place to put down his china so he went back into the kitchen and replaced it on the cleared table. The photograph was no longer there. Upstairs he could hear Julia taking to the man and woman. He stood undecided at the sink and looked again into the garden, to where the group had lain in the grass, and seeing nothing turned and went up the narrow stairs, under the wooden angel nailed to the wall, and saw Stanley holding his gun in the crook of his arm.

'I see you shoot, old man.'

'Not really. At one time my eldest son and I had a target up in the garden, but I rarely bother now.'

'Bit different from the weapons we had in the war, eh?' Stanley looked at Claud to see if they had a regiment to share, but Claud did not answer. The last time he had handled the gun had been that morning Maggie returned to London. He held his hand out and took the gun from Stanley and went to the window.

'Oh, Claud, not now, darling,' said Julia, 'you'll wake the baby.'

'It's all right, girl, it's not loaded.' He pushed wide the window and pressed the gun to his shoulder and looked along the line of the barrel. A tree, two trees, a patch of grass, a tub of marigolds, a rusted frame of a child's tricycle, a statue, headless, with one arm held out. He took aim and pulled the trigger, as he had that early morning when Shebah had been in the garden, and fired an imaginary bullet at the statue.

'It's quite well made,' he told Stanley, straightening up and placing the gun along the piano top, carefully, so as not to dislodge any of the numerous ornaments. 'It's remarkably accurate for its type.'

'Is it capable of killing?' asked Stanley, thereby eliminating any idea that he might have served in the Gunners.

'No. No, it's not capable of killing,' said Claud, and shut the window. He stood staring down at the piano top, sucking at the strands of beard that clung to his mouth. 'It is capable of making a wound though. It will establish contact with the flesh.'

Another pause, during which Betty sat motionless on the large sofa with her hands folded in her lap. For some reason she wanted to keep her wedding ring hidden from view. His view. The man at the window. Accordingly she put the fingers of her right hand about those of her left, covering the thin band of gold.

'It does establish reality,' Claud continued, 'a precise acoustical reality that one can hardly ignore.' He went and sat on the arm of the sofa, close to Betty, and frankly smiled down into her face.

'Are you happy, girl?' Again his arm went about her shoulders and quickly, to avoid talking to him so intimately, she asked Julia:

'May I see the photograph again, I didn't get a proper look at it?' and was grateful to Julia for joining her on the sofa and showing her the little square of card with the four strangers grouped together. 'Who is that?' she asked, pointing at the figure on the left of the picture. Whoever it was he seemed a little isolated from the others and his face was indistinct.

'That was Edward, the one that was going to marry Maggie. He was awfully nice. Quiet but very nice.'

'Awfully quiet and awfully nice,' echoed Claud, and quickly to avoid his comments Betty asked Julia:

'And who is that . . . that old woman on the chair?'

'That's Shebah. A friend of Maggie's. It's a very typical pose. She won't tell anyone how old she is and she's devoted to Maggie really though they fight all the time.'

Betty looked at the girl who thought she had been pregnant. She wasn't very much to look at with that beaked nose and the untidy hair. Did they mean she had been having a baby only she had taken something, or just that she had been mistaken? She wondered how long and in what way Claud had known her and had he sat often with his arm about her shoulders asking her if she was happy. Had he met her perhaps when she came to the shop and had it begun like today had begun? Probably not. She didn't look like the kind of person who could afford to buy anything.

Julia said: 'And that one is Norman. Everyone calls him Victorian Norman, because he wears round high collars and Maggie says he's Victorian. I don't know why really. He works in a factory and lives in the room above Maggie. At least he did until Maggie moved away. He doesn't like to say how old he is either. I don't know why because he's only young.'

She bent her head and peered through her spectacles at the recorded image of Victorian Norman. It was him and yet it was not him at all, she decided. He was dressed as he should be with the high rounded collar framing his face, and his Chelsea boots were just visible in the grass, but it was in the end only a photograph and lifeless. She bent closer and imagined that the nostrils of his nose were flaring slightly, that he was about to laugh in the manner peculiar to him alone....

Victorian Norman

In a decent society we should all be pushed to the wall. If not shot, then put outside the confines of the city, to roam like wolves in the great wastes beyond the gates. I might be salvaged were I to deny my friendship with them, having held a Union card for so long, or equally I could turn informer. Parasites I could say, clinging leech-like to the firm skin of the State. Hardly Shebah, I suppose, with her determination not to recognise the Welfare State, but emotionally she is a parasite.

Certain persons in the factory, Jean's father, for one, might not have much to say in my defence:

'Courted my daughter for three years and not a word in all that time to me. Working on the bench right next to the man and not even a nod of the head. The wife gave him Sunday lunch every Wednesday night for three years and still he never spoke. Got some flat in the city where he takes our Jean for weekends. Also his hair is too long and his manner of dressing is odd. When somebody's mother dies on the telly he usually laughs.'

And of course there is my persistent record of refusal to do overtime. I could plead there were factors outside my control that made it impossible to break with my undesirable friends. I would in the end survive. There might even be more opportunities open to me now, were I to return to conformity. To give expression to my affection for Maggie I appear to be 'one of them'. I have only gradually come to understand the difference between myself and these others. They have broken the tape of environment emotionally whereas I have accomplished it mentally. Which leaves me free to return to harbour whenever I choose. Maggie left home very early, in a wild stampede of open revolt, splintering in the process the whole framework of her background, so that she finds now with grief that she has nothing to return to but the ruins. I spent ten years preparing my family for my departure. At thirty years of age I at last lifted the brass knocker of the house in Morpeth Street. When I entered and put my corporeal body fair and square into the dark interior of the now familiar hall, I shivered with delight. The shiver of the natural swimmer who had not till this moment known the exact location of the river. With Maggie gone, nothing has altered, save that she has gone. When I think of her, which I do some part of every day, it is with seriousness. There have been so many words we have spoken to each other. In one day I almost see her a dozen times in the street. Sometimes it is the line of her jaw, sometimes a lank length of hair lying across the velvet collar of a coat. I am always surprised at what I feel when I actually come face to face with her. For one thing there are brown stains on her teeth from too much smoking and for another I had forgotten how parched are her lips. Her whole mouth puckers with dryness. When she looks at me, which she did just a moment ago, not smiling but with intensity, I want to laugh. I can feel my mouth begin to tremble at the edges. She is trying to tell me that I alone understand, which I don't, and even if I did the effect is somewhat spoiled by having watched her look just as intently at almost everyone. Indiscriminate intensity of manner. Also I am disillusioned by her to an extent that I find remarkable, as I did not intend to have illusions. When in the beginning she called me her rock of ages, I did not suppose I would become a rock. When she constantly referred to my qualities of steadfastness and my integrity I did not comprehend that it was her feminine way of obscuring the fact she felt no desire for me. The advantages have only slightly outweighed the frustrations. It has meant I could watch her undress for bed, that I could soap her back, her faintly sallow back curved over the plastic bowl in the sink, and that I could keep track of her bimestrial attachments. On occasions I could be her petal, her gold flower, her dulce boy, her jewel. Indiscriminate tenderness, indiscernible from the real thing, so that lulled by her glucose endearments, my fingers slippery with soap, a shoal of little fishes would begin a shy glissade over the surface of her damp and bony ribs, sliding upwards, would flicker in and out between her globy breasts, only to find that in a moment the golden boy, the petal boy would be banished utterly and the man of rock called upon. The towel draped about her chest for protection, she would extol my many virtues, rubbing herself dry the while, edging sideways and with decorum into the all-enveloping folds of her cherry dressing gown, leaving me alone at the sink with outstretched hands still damp with soap, outmanoeuvred to the last. It's true of course that I am Maggie's very own personal rock, that I can behave as spinelessly as I choose with other women, without damaging our relationship. It is true also that Maggie herself chooses endlessly and unerringly to become involved with men who lack totally those steadfast qualities she so admires in me. At the moment the thoughtful Edward, sitting there on the grass with shoulders hunched, looks the exception to the rule, but then he hasn't known Maggie very long and the foundations of his character have not yet been exposed to her full and merciless attentions. It is to be hoped that the little frown between his brows is caused by the glare of the sunlight, or the smoke from his cigarette, and not by any uneasiness he may be feeling due to the frequent disappearances of Maggie throughout the long night. I could lean forward and whisper my congratulations in his ear, if only to enjoy the astonishment blossoming on his pleasant face. It is not given to us all to achieve fatherhood so quickly or so effortlessly. And if Maggie's choice was made in haste, at least he was chosen. If he is an honourable man there may even be a wedding. Shebah can be both bridesmaid and Godmother, and Claud will be best man. The sun will shine and Maggie will hold flowers against her bulging waistline, and with any luck I shall be left alone with the gentle Julia.

The tragedy of Claud and Maggie lies in the regularity of their non-conformity. Everything being permissible they are lost to the delights of the unpermitted. Julia and I, not being so emancipated, can appreciate to the full the bitter-sweet flavour of infidelity. In the brief tiled seclusion of the bathroom last night she struggled rapturously to remove my hands from the buttons of her blouse. From her armpits came the seed cake smell of the virtuous female.

Shebah being here this weekend has partially spoiled my enjoyment. In the confines of the kitchen in Morpeth Street she is sufficiently restricted to be cautious. Her discretion guarantees that she remains once weekly in her wickerwork chair by the cupboard. But the air here, and the trees and the flowers, not to mention the pride-swelling injury to her leg, may well unhinge her. Accustomed as she has been all these years to perpetual vistas of chimneys black with soot and a day by day denial of her existence by a hostile world, she could not be blamed for growing lyrical about this experience. It is not often one spends a weekend in the country. If she so far forgets herself as to let slip some echo of this visit to Jean when next they meet, how shall I counteract her words? The business of lying extensively is exhausting and robs the deceit of its bloom.

For Maggie the truth itself is a lie. She will tell Edward, if she has not already done so, that Claud's rifle fire this morning was meant for him. 'Because, you see, Edward,' she will tell him, not for a moment allowing him to turn away from the consummate eloquence of her tender eyes, 'he loves me, he always has.' I must admit I am curious to know for whom the shot was intended. I cannot believe that Claud is an inferior marksman, so I cannot believe that he aimed at Shebah. It is possible that he fired at me, angry at my evening-long attention to his mistress, and that she, the sane and loyal Julia, seeing him bulky in the open window of the upstairs room, flew like a bird whilst his finger already whitened on the trigger, and jerked his elbow outward. The reality of the shot is established, though the identity of the victim is unknown. I cannot believe that Claud cares enough about Shebah to wound her. Only Shebah and Maggie care that much about Shebah. Maggie thinks Shebah unique and magnificent in her arrogance. If I am her golden boy, her petal boy, then Shebah is her diamond brain. Her magnificence Maggie attributes to her temperament and her race. I ascribe it to the abscence of her ovaries. An insistently expressed egotism is the keynote of the hypogonad character. Coupled with and dependent on this is an active resentment towards a world that is inadequately mindful of her imagined excellences. Give Shebah back her ovaries and Maggie would cease to find her interesting. As to her arrogance being in any way racial, in all history only the Jews went so patiently and so gently to the slaughter.

Between Maggie and Shebah lies distance measured in years. Between Maggie and I there is a distance that is due to the difference in our sex. There are of course other kinds of distance that are calculable. There is a distance between people caused by the class system, that is measurable. The sun is about ninety-three million miles away mathematically. Visually it is just behind that tree and a little below that cloud. Maggie is much nearer and Shebah is so close that I can feel against my shoulder blade, her spatulate bare toe protruding from her openwork sandal, irritably jigging up and down. She would probably like to give me a strong kick in the back of the neck, just where it joins my frail spinal column, and pitch me forward on to my nose, but then she has to pretend that she is weak from loss of blood. Not that she bled at all, or if she did it was internal bleeding and not for the eye to see. Consequently I cannot give her the sympathy that may be justly hers. Everything depends on other factors. For instance I am only sprawled here on the grass in all this heat because it is summer. It is a seasonal sprawling. Also if it were not Whitsun or Bank Holiday or whatever it is, I would be at the factory. And if I were not Maggie's best friend I should not have been invited to spend the weekend at Claud's, he being Maggie's best friend. We are all best friends and it is not a limited company. I would not be here if it was winter. It might be snowing and to lie face downwards in the white drifts would be eccentric.

Claud probably does just that, all winter long, searching with his microscopic eyes for signs of life. He is going through his good earth phase, just as last year or the year before he underwent his religious revival. His pre-Julia existence. Across his lemon pale face continually flitted the expression of a man in search of God. 'I cannot give you the whole,' he said, 'I can only give you a part.' He blended perfectly into the purple sofa in Maggie's living room. The candle in its brass holder dripped wax on to the brick hearth and garlands of coloured paper, put up for Christmas and long since forgotten, cross-crossed in loops of orange and blue above his saintly head. His head was saintly merely in its appearance; the abundant hair, haloed faintly by the candle-light that flickered above the sofa back, the yellow beard in tendrils about his dewy mouth, the eyelids bosselated by hidden eyes. For all his study of the Bible his encephalic cavities still strove with fleshling thoughts. He constantly told Maggie she ought to cleave to him and become one. Once he woke in the middle of the night, in spite of his double dose of sleep-inducing pills, and pissed with a high cavatina of sound into the Victorian chamber pot that stood on the small table beside the brass bed. The pot being full of dried earth, hard as rock, could not absorb his offering and the liquid spilled on to the wooden floor, waking Maggie, who in the light of the still burning candles saw him on tip-toe, bunching himself in his two hands, the shadow of his body huge across the fireplace wall, a drunken dancer tripping the light fantastic. The chamber pot belonged originally to the mother of the Wild Colonial Boy. When he returned to collect his pictures and his brass horn and his boxing gloves, he would also have taken his pot but for the geranium stub embedded in clay. The removal men responsible for the safe conduct of Maggie's effects dropped the pot going down the grey stone steps. The fall cracked the chamber neatly into two halves and dislodged the lump of earth. They swept the halves of china into a refuse bin, but the clod lay for two days on the pavement. I did hope a shower of rain might miraculously revive it, but the twig stayed dead, and crumbled into dust.

'How sad,' said Maggie, when I told her, without real depth of emotion. Set all round this courtyard, in Grecian urns and tubs bound with copper, Claud has grown a multitude of plants whose name I do not begin to know. Claud himself hardly knew a few months ago, before his fervour for the soil began.

'You know where you are, cocker,' he informed me last night, 'when you plant a seed.'

Now there, he and Edward should have room for discussion.

Julia, every morning, draped in a dressing gown of grenadine silk, waters each pot with deliberate care. Had I so far forgotten myself this weekend as to return the compliment and urinate into one of the stone urns bedecked with blossom, Claud would doubtless have shot me along with Shebah. His eyes continually widen in their search for decay that may suddenly appear upon his precious leaves. The plants themselves give off a purely chemical aroma, besprayed as they are from dawn till dusk with insecticide.

Last night the head gardener in his bathrobe of many colours spent some time with his spray, having made sure beforehand that I would not employ my time in his absence pursuing Julia. It meant that I spent a restless night on the couch with the dog for company, whilst Claud refreshed by his night-air administrations noisily attended to his other flower, his gentle budlet released from her glass spectacles, her buttoned blouse, lying tender amid the lavender sheets of the ornate bed. It is only of small comfort to imagine that perhaps she thought of me minutely whilst undergoing her Claudian atrocities. Twice Julia came to Morpeth Street. Once in spring and again in winter. In the spring Claud had cut her hair and she wore a cream-coloured skirt that she washed without fail every one of the three nights of their stay. In winter she had a cold that tinged her nostrils a tender pink and her hair grown long was in a bun at the nape of her neck. The sight of her white, her glossy hyaline neck caused Maggie to scrub hers for several nights afterwards with her toothbrush in an attempt to remove some of the ingrained dirt.

'Did you see it,' she asked me unnecessarily, 'like milk, Norman? Honest to God, like a glass of milk.'

When I saw this weekend the dapper tiles and shining taps in Claud's bathroom it became abundantly clear why Julia has a neck that is lily pale. The bathroom in Morpeth Street holds no usable bath. There is a copper geyser that sags outwards like a disused tea-urn, and a faint smell of gas forever in the air. Less privileged guests slept on the divan under the window and emerged the next morning, unless fortunate enough to be suffering from insomnia, partially poisoned by fumes. I myself went home on a Tuesday, and still do, to bath. Maggie, having the children, had to make do at the sink.

Looking at her now she does not appear to be unhappy, but then it is not at all apparent that she has any capacity for happiness. When she falls into my arms my laugh becomes a spasm. She frequently tells me my sound for laughing is absurd. I do not know how otherwise to give vent to my feelings when she lies so close to my heart. My laugh is in its way like the length of my hair, so repugnant to my family, a deliberate eccentricity. It is not so much a sign of comical relaxation as a method of releasing excitement. Thus when the shop bell rang its angelus yesterday morning, and Claud with weary eyes held out his arms to enfold his soul-mate, I laughed with elation, sensing the coming confusion. The small white teeth of Claud bit softly into the extruded lower lip that Maggie laid against his mouth. Only the voice of Shebah raised in extreme complaint as her foot was crushed, invaded their intimacy. With well-bred patience Edward stood and seemed not to see the embrace. The temperature of the shop rose slightly with our entrance. A gentle flush suffused the rounded cheeks of the mild Julia.

Maggie had told me often about the house, about all the pictures, about the harp and the beds of French design, about the cupids holding up the many lamps. But I had not comprehended what it would be like visually when I saw it for myself. Like a salvo from a gong the laden rooms sent out their shimmering waves as Claud, talking with the accents of one who constantly rehearses his role, led us to the upstairs room. Maggie, childlike in her delight, stood with legs well apart, puckering her nose; surprisingly dimples appeared in the drawn face, the phosphor eyes shone emotionally. Shebah, her face struggling to preserve its tragic mask, let fall her bags upon the sofa. That Edward failed to share our excitement was to be expected. For him the room, packed like a bazaar, was only another room and not a plateau of historical importance. Here, Claud had unfurled his flags of domestic war, begat his numerous children, there on the rug before the open hearth, in winter and in summer. Here, the immortal Billie had spoken to Maggie for the last time, trailing his fingers across the strings of the lurching harp. Claud, hitherto the chief clown in his frock coat of Indian origin, worn on his circus visits to Morpeth Street, now came into his own element, out of the sawdust ring and into the glittering arena of antiquity, the dealer in furniture, the man of property. He wagged his bearded head with pleasure at our appreciation. He informed us that the kettle was on to make tea and that we really must see his roses. Shebah and he eyed each other with veiled welcome. They became the oldest opposites in the world. Time without number, under every conceivable circumstance, what they would say to each other had been said.

'Well, Shebah.' It was not a question, only a greeting. Enacting a ritual, though she has never been here before, and never will return. Shebah raised her arms, the palms of her hands turned to the ceiling. Well pleased with each other they laughed. All the time Claud did not really take his attention away from Edward, standing placidly beside the piano. He watched Edward's hand search for his cigarettes and only when he had lit one and begun to inhale did Claud move forward to offer him one of his own.

'No, no, thank you,' said Edward, 'I've got one.' He fumbled again in his pocket. 'Have one of mine.'

'No, old boy, I prefer these,' and having accomplished something, though what, Edward will never know, Claud returned to Shebah. Through an open door in another room Julia told Maggie how well she is looking. Julia is mistaken though not insincere. When I saw Maggie at the station I too thought she looked well. Only on the bus journey did I begin to observe, like a picture coming into focus, the signs of exhaustion on her face. Billie asked me in the kitchen that May night if I did not think she had deteriorated physically. He leant his arms on the table and stared at me, part bewildered, part aggressive. Only having seen Maggie constantly I could not understand him. Now after this passage of time it is conceivable that he was right. It is also plausible that she has never looked healthy, that her febrile features are a matter of inheritance.

'I did love her, you know, Norman,' said Billie, emphasising with his fist the past tense of declaration. He rested his burning cheek on the oilcloth of the table. As he repeated his statement his mouth rumpled, the dry surface of his underlip clung to the cloth. Across the bald crown of his head the shadow fringe of the light shade swung back and forth.

'I just couldn't bear the mess, Norman. I just couldn't get used to the dirt everywhere. Not just the children's things, but when I opened cupboards and a pile of soiled clothes and paint rags fell out. And all the furniture was falling to pieces. Backs off chairs and handles off the doors, and all the time she kept up this pretence of not being aware of it. I could never win an argument, never. She had an answer to everything. She had this dreadful capacity for making me feel petty, for being so bloody strong about everything. A flood of words and ideas and twisting me round and round till I wanted to just run. It was her self-deception that finished me, I simply couldn't compete. I hadn't the words. The funny thing was that when I went home to my mother's for the weekend, the tidiness there got on my nerves. And Maggie used to gloat over that. I kept watching my mother cook beautiful meals and hearing Maggie say how degraded women became through housework and how the only important thing was the mind. And I could see that my mother's mind wasn't all that stimulating, but she did cook eatable food, and I couldn't decide which in the end was most important to my well-being. The food or the mind. I wanted it to be the mind, I really did, but I just couldn't change.' He looked sideways at me; the blue eyes rolled up, leaving a blind curve of milky eyeball. It was evident that talking about it made him more undecided than ever. 'You see, there wasn't any happy medium. It was all discussion and probing and burnt bacon...' His voice faltered and stopped against the cool surface of the plastic cloth. After a moment he said:

'The awful thing is that if only she had washed a bit more and looked a bit prettier and cooked just a bit better, I'd have married her. I really would. Was I wrong, Norman? Was I really wrong?'

Maggie pressed me to tell her every word we spoke together. I omitted to tell her my response to the tamed Colonial Boy. I would have lied had I told him he was wrong. Besides he did not wish to be told that, being so convinced that he was. The large lobe of his ear buckled on the table top. Even the hairs in the cavity of his ear were bleached by the sun.

'You've no idea, Norman,' he said, 'what it's like out there. The sun and the showers and the clean streets and air you can breathe and no dirt anywhere. There just isn't room for any dirt.'

By now the bloom will have faded from his skin. The new clothes, along with the traumatic check coat, will have frayed at the cuffs, a line of grease will encircle the insides of his collars. Bowler hatted and city white, the rugby forward calves swelling in his panaloons, he will be again the untidy lubberly boy that Maggie knew. If he worked on the assumption, false, that he was safe if he moved for cover before the explosion, he will know better now. It had already happened to him; the bang did not herald his destruction, merely followed after. Clutching his pictures, dangling his boxing gloves, he stumbled into the night, a man partially restored. I did not think it worth while to tell him of the atomy being he had deposited with Maggie, the apodixis of his own disorder, later to become no doubt Edward's joy, his angelet in a dark and naughty world.

Last night Edward twice left the table around which we sat in Claud's kitchen to see if the children were safe. Boyishly he excused himself, laying a nicotine stained hand across the grateful shoulders of his lady love. Shebah, clutching her spotted handkerchief, the receptacle for her frequent and ecstatic tears, played to the full her role of purity, the spiritual being among the crowd of debauchees.

'I think you're all terrible, darlings,' she cried, rolling her eyes like a stag at bay, forking heaped quantities of cottage pie into her starved and painted mouth.

'I reckon,' said Claud, not intending to sound American, 'that we're more to be pitied than envied.'

'Pitied?' She almost choked with her indignation. 'Pitied, with you all getting what you bloody well want?'

'I reckon we never get what we want. None of us ever has.'

Edward, moving on his hard chair, looked quickly at Maggie and away again.

'Oh, I don't know, darling. Life's not so bad.' With a belly full of trouble Maggie tried to minimise the implication in Claud's remark. 'We do have a lot of fun.' She laughed and leaned her head against the broad shoulder of her best friend Edward. 'I should have worn my hat,' she murmured, 'the one I wore at my father's funeral. You remember the night Liz got attacked in the street and there was a fog and no one could go home...' She lapsed into silence. It was either she felt genuine sorrow at the thought of her dead Daddy or she didn't want Edward to know about the bedding arrangements that night.

'Oh, darling,' said Shebah. 'I remember so well. Your poor dead father.' Unable to resist the opportunity afforded for criticism she said ... 'Mrs Ryan had to stay the night. She slept in the brass bed, didn't she? I seemed to be required to rest on the couch. Not that I got any sleep with you singing away in the kitchen as if you'd come from a wedding. Such an odd way of expressing respect for the departed.' She smiled wildly as if to take the sting out of her words. Strangely, of us all, her face alone bears the stamp of depravity. Her mouth hangs down in a plum-ripe lobe of obscenity. The exodus of Edward and his birthday mate caused her to grimace as if in pain. A thin scream of protest exploded in her teeming brain. Claud, knowing full well the havoc it would wreak upon her temperamental nervous system, quietly refilled her glass. His eyes were beamy with arch mischief. Despite this he managed to be aware that my hand under the heavy table caressed the linen-covered thigh of his Julia. His professional eye lit up at contact with a situation not entirely distasteful to him. Secure in his knowledge of me he raised the gloomy Shebah to her white sandalled feet and led her away. Thoughtfully he stroked the springing hairs of his beard, head a little on one side, watching me standing openly at the sink with my arm about Julia. She hardly knew what to do, but made a great show of washing the dishes. In honey-thick tones of disapproval Shebah asked to be allowed to assist with the washing up. She had no intention of doing so, she merely wished to let me know that once and for all I was a libertine. Her voice going upstairs was heavy with annoyance, her vowels were laden with feeling, a showy sigh preceded each step of the way.

Hot steam had misted Julia's glasses. Under my arm the narrow shoulders were stooped. Caught in a spasm of laughter I removed her spectacles and like a bird with beak open for food, almost blind, she protested ... 'O, Norman' ... and in the protest I kissed her mouth, not heavily but lightly, because I was not sure of her reaction. When I had wiped her glasses clean I replaced them on the bridge of her polished nose. Her hand came up to settle them more firmly leaving a smear of soap across the smoothness of her cheek. It is in little things that I find extremes of excitement, the erotica of the wholly ordinary explored to its furthermost limits, so that I found a ravishment of sensation in the near-sighted blinking of her eyes. When I had taken off her apron, worn to protect her linen skirt, I put my pinnyless little Julia on my lap, sitting on a chair by the table, and we talked. The conversation was as usual about Maggie, well away in the guest room making a father out of the unsuspecting Edward. I have found in these three years that I am endlessly involved in discussions upon Maggie, about her past, her present, her unpredictable future.

'What if Edward thinks it a bit strange—her being pregnant so quickly? What if he doesn't want to marry her?' She was really concerned; the soft mouth quivered with compassion. 'What if the baby looks like Billie?'

Claud has taught her nothing it seems, which is in part her charm. Maggie and I have already talked about the possibility of a Billie baby and found it amusing. In infantile form the Wild Colonial Boy clenches his tiny fists with hunger. To console Julia I drew her closer to me. I was happy enough to be content with stroking her hand, lying on the surface of the table. A little hand with polished nails, curved like a soft paw under my fingers. With Julia I find my delights belong to the primary school. My first Best Friend, please sit by me, you can drink my milk if you like. A moist flash of emotion, a lisping turn of phrase, an adorable secret to be whispered into an adorable ear. The realisation that to Claud and for Claud she is a big grown-up girl only accentuates my pleasure. Safe in my arms she snuggled against me, able to be confiding.

'I envy her, you know. I do really, Norman. Yes honestly I do.' Honestly and with envy the little hand moved in my palm. 'Of course it wouldn't be the same for Claud, a baby I mean.' Her mouth against my cheek opened in a little gush of laughter, causing her to squirm on my knee. Her breath smelled warm, smoky, the pointed tongue flickered out between the even teeth and withdrew again. Upstairs Shebah's laugh stuttered out, like a stick dragged at speed across railings, and terminated abruptly. With the laugh and the silence and the warmth of the little kitchen clean as an apple, without so much as the ticking of a clock, the world flew on.

Though I do not believe in God, despising with true party fervour this opium of the people, I am wrapped deep in childhood bands of Sunday school faith. That I am mortal, meaning doomed to die, does not, like Shebah, cause me to be in mourning for my life. When I climb my mountains I am intensely aware of my healthy body breathing air purified by height, and were I to receive some warning of impending death I would most certainly lift up mine eyes unto the hills, and though as a Marxist I would be conscious of the puerile sentiments of my dying mind, as a sensualist I could only sink down on my carnal knees with heartfelt praise. The little things that hold me close to the centre of my own universe fling Maggie into the void. I hold no illusions as to my usefulness in the social scheme of things. That I work for a fair wage does not mean that privately I contribute constructively to anything but my own shadow. I am a blind one-dimensional nonentity in a pipe-dream paradise. I more than accept the realisation of my own unreality whereas Claud and Maggie and the biologically tormented Shebah wrestle day long, life long, in a ludicrous attempt to tear the stars down from the sky and bring them within reach of their destructive fingers. That they never succeed only darkens their blood and proceeds to do any amount of damage to their overloaded brains. It would not surprise me if Maggie died of an explosion in the head, eyes charred in their sockets, features contorted with agony, whereas I shall merely fall into a profound sleep and only a pocket mirror held to my composed lips will show that my lungs have ceased to function. Likewise my little Julia. In the kitchen I received nothing and everything from her inhibited being. That is to say I was given in abundance the sweet smell of her hair and skin, the trusting proximity of her body, the dulcimer tones of her ladylike voice.

'You are so understanding, Norman. You are so nice.'

Nicely I squeezed her waist in appreciation and nicely my head spun in a fox-trot of titillation. After a while, because the unseen Claud in the room above was not conducive to relaxation, I suggested we go into the garden. Not wasteful of time Julia took a bucket from under the sink and filled it at the tap, in preparation for watering Claud's thirsty roses. We are one flesh, my love and I. His roses are my roses. In mild jealousy I sat at the garden table and watched her attend to his plants. Shebah's shadow in time to music crossed the yard. The gramophone was probably driving her to a pitch of distraction that would end in Claud's annihilation. Her face this morning, when she was shot, drooped in an hilarious parody of pain. I do not doubt that she was shocked but I could not help laughing as I uncrumpled her much crumpled body. A face of *papier-mâché* with eyes of Indian ink lolling against my arm. So often, taking her home at night, has she suddenly flung her arm across her eyes and leant against the pillars of some house. The catonic pose would be held until, sensitive to what was proper, she would let loose a groan of funereal depth. Having heard wolf cried so often and so loudly I am no longer able to make the appropriate sounds of sympathy.

Once only have I been stirred by her dilemma, occasioned by the arrival, unexpected, of a German professor, come in hopes of courting Maggie. A kitchenful of people made his mouth droop in absurd disappointment, but we gave him chips in a little folder of newspaper and Maggie, face shining with mock hospitality and that particular animation that makes her glow lantern bright, sat close to him so that in a little while he was all smiles and eager-beaver politeness. But the little room was so hot and so squalid in its dimensions that the conversation became more personal. The professor, grey flannel trousers impossibly wide at the ankle, perspiration running into his candid eyes, was asked about East Germany. The plump hand that was in the act of forking fried potatoes into his mouth was arrested in mid-air. Foolishly he stared at us over the pronged vegetable, blinking rapidly as if the upper part of his face had been caught in a high wind. Attempting to articulate, his lips twitched to form words.

'It is inhuman,' he told us, 'a system not to my liking.'

Shebah moved sullenly in her wicker chair.

'Now in West Germany'—and here his hand, the one still holding the forked potato, jabbed at the surface of the snow-cemmed brick wall as if to point a geographical position—'we are free.'

My mind in all its automatic record player glory began to repeat its party lines.

'You Germans have always been a materialistic race, along with the rest of Europe, but you are distinguished mainly for your efficiency.'

At this his bland face rumpled and a drop of salty distillation slid from the lobe of his right ear on to the blue table top.

'I do not follow you. How so are we efficient?'

'In your method of killing,' said Maggie, who knows my line of argument even better than myself. All the time she looked fixedly, as if into a crystal, at the little globe of sweat upon the cloth. In Nuremberg gloom we shifted on our chairs until the little Jewish judge dressed all in black, disorientated beyond repair through ovarian loss, opened her crimson crinose lips and spat into the silence—

'Six million of my people in the gas oven, darling.'

Alone we might have retorted that Shebah had never seen anyone inside a gas oven except perhaps the gas man, but the presence of the German from Berlin kept us silent. He, thrown as he was by the endearment wrapped round the handle of the knife, stared at us without courage. Then Shebah, seeing the little frantic movement of his agitated adam's apple, smiled her small persecuted smile and said: 'Oh, it's nothing personal, darling'—and allowed us to begin to restore the evening. For the rest of the night, though, she sat without speech, hands clutching her black bag stuffed with documents, weighed down with a massive melancholy. Then, yes then, I did feel sorry for her. To be always missing the crucifixion one craves, to be allied but isolated from a race that has suffered. To wait for ever for a Messiah that never comes. That is why Claud's accidental, and it was surely that, gun wound has become for me an action of abundant charity. Shebah herself might have preferred a near death attack with attendant blood transfusions and bunches of grapes, but then beggars cannot choose. Hearing her voice from where I sat in the shadowy garden last night raised high in complaint and demented laughter one would have thought she was intent on butchering Claud. The house guest turned violent. Julia, watering the roses, one arm gleaming palely in the dusk, glanced now and then at the open window. A fluted giggle escaped her composed lips.

'She sounds so cross.'

In mock protection I rose and put my arm about her waist. She was too kind to draw away from me abruptly and besides the wine drunk in large quantities throughout the evening was having a liberating effect upon her.

There were two things jostling in my mind. Whether it was nobler to suffer the slings and arrows of an outraged Claud or be content with a gentle embracing beyond the yard and in the long grass of the little perfumed garden. I have found with women that nothing is predictable. The most natural seeming conquest can turn into a virago of puritanism and the most shy suddenly a changeling of delicious eagerness. The worry was where to conduct my exploratory advances with some semblance of dignity. Claud's particular form of humour would delight in spying me beneath some tree in a crucial state of undress. Had I known last night about his predilection for firing guns into the undergrowth I should never have debated. In the end it was Julia who solved the problem by suggesting innocently that she show me the barn, which lay at right angles to the house, containing Claud's larger treasures. To the accompaniment of shouts and groans from Shebah on her psychiatric couch in the consulting room above the shop, Julia unlocked the wooden door and switched on the light. With the tremor of air caused by the door closing behind us, a gigantic female torso, a ship's figurehead of nautical desire, swung gently above our heads suspended from the roof by almost invisible hawsers. Ah, God, to be thus exposed to such a mammoth piece of timber curved in mammiferous splendour. Red mouth set in a salt sea smile, she swayed her ballooning breasts across the barn. Tiny cracks like veins ran along the varnished apples of her cheeks. Her nippled shadow sliced across the furniture piled beneath her. Tables, chairs, sofas, cabinets, in long rows clear to the end of the barn and between the rows narrow corridors of space, along one of which Julia began to walk. Though I had to relinquish my hold on her waist I could admire the round little buttocks moving in front of me.

It is a pity I have not been able to tell Maggie about last night, the situation being so dramatic. A film set, a dream fantasy concocted by Claud, ever the ideal host, with sofas and divans on every side of me, and my marine arcadian beauty flying aloft, and my little Julia stepping ahead of me, a small pallid ear on either side of her round neat head, and a dozen hair clips sliding from her soft blown hair.

At the far end of the barn I made the beautiful discovery that the building was L-shaped, that there was a little avenue of sofas on our left, almost in darkness. In particular there was one sofa upholstered in green velvet with a gilt curved back and a seat as wide as a small divan. I could not take my eyes off its dim orchard depths. The figurehead, now out of sight, had constricted my throat; I sat down on the velvet sofa hardly able to breathe and listened to the loud uneven beating of my heart. Julia was busily examining a small table, presumably for signs of woodworm, peering at its surface through short-sighted eyes with disproportionate interest. Her arm, raised to touch the wood, hid entirely the docile bosom buttoned beneath the silken blouse.

'Oh, look, Norman,' she said with gentle dismay, 'a little hole—just here—and look, another one.' Eyebrows high with alarm she stroked the damaged wood. I was afraid her concern would make her run at once to fetch Claud so I left my sofa and inspected the table, though I couldn't see anything, but at least I had my arm round her waist. I kept remembering what Maggie had told me on various occasions, that a woman will always know when she is about to be molested, and even if she doesn't like you she will have difficulty in breathing, though the cause must not be confused with passion. I could not really tell whether Julia was breathing normally or not because I could hear nothing above the thudding of my own heart, so Maggie's advice was in itself of little use, but I did know she liked me and I remembered how little time there was, then as now, or ever, and pulled her round to face me and kissed her. I don't think she was very responsive but a middle-class upbringing is a great help. If you have been taught that a refusal will cause offence and that politeness is next to Godliness then you don't push a house guest away in a hurry. At least Julia didn't and somehow, with a great deal of loud exhalations on my part and a variety of kittenish mewings from her, I contrived to reach my goal, my green savannah, my velvet sofa in the gloom, and place her upon it. I had to keep her upon it by sheer force, not by my arms exactly but rather a strong pressure of my mouth against hers, which was more painful than exciting, but at least it was something. The wine had made me light-headed and we both seemed to be trapped under glass, inside a vacuum, and I couldn't hear a thing save for the muffled drum beat in my ears. And I had a picture in my mind of her little soft paps limp and rose-tipped crushed against my shirt and her thighs pressed close together and in the middle of my thinking she suddenly stopped resisting and lay more or less inert along the green sofa. I cannot say she was willing. More likely, as Maggie would no doubt tell me, it was only she had decided to get it over as quickly as possible. She lay with her eyes closed tight, arms crossed meekly over her buttoned blouse, spectacles awry on the bridge of her sharp little nose. I kept my eyes on her face all the time I removed my clothes behind the sofa. I can undress more rapidly than most. I don't even care to leave my socks on. I didn't care about Julia being fully clothed if she preferred it but I wanted nothing between me and the cool surfaces of her little protesting hands but my skin, faintly goose-pimpling with the chill air. As I straightened up in a quiver of energy, bare to the elements, ready to spring upon my hostess with the tightly closed eyes, pausing only a moment to stretch the toe of my right foot, numb from the constriction of a Chelsea boot, I saw a little window half-obscured by creeper that I had not seen before, and outside the glass, blurred only fractionally, the sardonic face of Claud. Shock momentarily paralysed me. Only my big toe, crushed yellow like a flower left between the pages of a book, moved sideways and back in an attempt to restore circulation. Then my reflexes saved me and jerkily like an old film running backwards I re-dressed again watched by the smiling face without. I could not really see the smile on Claud's features but knowing him I could imagine it. When Julia opened her eyes I was fixing my tie. Puzzled but infinitely relieved she adjusted her glasses and raised herself from the sofa and resumed her inspection of the worm-afflicted table. If she felt any confusion she showed no sign of it and one hand domestically secured the few remaining clips in her hair.

'Norman,' she said after only a moment, 'I do think I should tell Claud about this table.'

I could only agree and single file we walked back along the narrow strip of barn, under the tethered goddess of the waves beneath whose briny breasts stood Claud, stroking his beard as always, underlip glistening with enjoyment from the repeated caresses of his tongue. Julia broke into a little run towards him, a little trip of speed to tell him about the decaying table. He nodded his head kindly and smiled all the time at me over the top of her neat and anxious head, and with an increased flurry of heart-beats I followed him out of the barn without a backward glance at my busty Madonna of the air. I waited whilst Julia relocked the heavy door, Claud standing by his roses, not touching them, just following the slight movement of the leaves as they bounced gently in the night breeze. I do wonder if he would have continued to watch through the small window had I not seen him. Knowing or rather not knowing Claud, it is possible. The thought is an erotic one, even more stimulating than the taking of the submissive Julia, and as we went into the house Claud laid his arm across my shoulders and squeezed my upper arm with his stubby fingers.

Shebah was sitting as if under sedatives in the living room, the two dogs at her feet, her hands folded on her lap. She gave me a look of hatred and then one of sweet reproach; the lover who has been wronged. Oh, my darling, how could you? Keep your mind on gas ovens, Shebah, my love.

Claud gave us all another drink, omitting Julia who had to ask for one, and he pretended not to hear. He then suggested that we should sing 'Happy Birthday' to Maggie and Edward. I almost felt that with his attention to detail he would show us a hole in the wall through which we might watch silently or otherwise the celebrating communicants within the name-day bedroom. But all we did was to stand bunched like a posy of assorted and un-named flowers outside the latched door and sing our greetings.

Inside, Maggie opened her chapped and curvy mouth to emit a ho-ho-ho of polite laughter. She is constantly trying to please, to win approval, to make amends. This I understand only because she has tried in part to explain it to me. She has gone to bed with numerous strangers rather than offend. It has constantly hurt that our own closeness has meant that she has been cruelly offensive to me. I could imagine her lying in the bed, encircled by the large and friendly hands of the placid Edward, her face split by a smile, eyes open, playing the eager acquiescer to an empty room filled only with darkness.

Claud did attempt to enter but Julia restrained him. Shebah surprisingly was trembling. The bracelets on her plump arms slithered with agitation; a pisiform gob of saliva shot forth from the purple linings of her crêpe cheeks as her mouth opened in a wide shout of laughter. Like Maggie the noise was a polite gesture though she may have been experiencing enjoyment. Still singing we returned to the living room to take up our positions. Julia sat in the large armchair and crossed her legs. Her hand came down to straighten her dress but she caught me looking at her and rubbed her knee instead. The titillation afforded at the thought of Maggie and Edward wantonly together in the guest room, coupled with her little adventure in the barn, so inconclusive to me, had made her coquettish. The warm breeze from the open window blew across her hair. She patted her head with a capable hand and touched her flushed cheeks. We were all for various reasons, or perhaps the same reason, in a state of elation. It was not only the drink because we had consumed enough by now to put us all in a melancholy stupor. Shebah, unable to sit still, thrust out her lower lip and blinked rapidly under the crystal chandelier. Posturing sternly she placed a grubby finger to her scarlet mouth and studied the oil painting above the fireplace. The pig-tailed head turned from side to side in near blind examination. Because I asked her, and because in the end nothing would stop her, she began to sing. She needed to exhaust herself in some way and without an outlet she might have engaged Julia in conversation. Performing a few steps of what may have been a minuet, bowing low to an invisible accompanist at the visible piano, she tripped formally about the glittering room, furry lip opening drowsily. As if better to observe her I slid to the floor and leant against the exposed knees of the seated Julia.

Absorbed in a vision of herself that was wholly music hall in origin, the red fingers bitten short scrabbling to lift her tight shirt higher, Shebah cavorted with corybantic fervour. Claud, ignoring this precocious child up long past her bedtime, weaved his way down the room, arms held out like a wrestler, to fetch another bottle from the cupboard. She misunderstood his mission for a moment and imagined he wished to partner her and tossed her head haughtily. At his avoidance her mouth crumpled like a rose falling apart. Claud's back expressed nothing at all. Maggie, had she been present, would have murmured how sad it all was. Claud's head in the cupboard might have been distorted with grief, tears stinging the lids of his blue and oceanic eyes, might, but more likely he smiled at the memory of me in the barn, naked, as his fingers closed round the slender bottle of Spanish wine. Behind him, skirt hitched high to where, if pigs could fly, there would have been a stitched and lacy garter, Shebah continued to entertain. Bidding a much-tried and now elderly lover to forgive and forget, lower lip impossibly drooping, now folding her squat arms bare to the elbow across her parched bosom, now flinging both arms wide to embrace his return, she filled the room with ascensional entreaty.

I felt comfortably at ease. Not for me the complicated subtleties of atmosphere that constantly assail Maggie. For myself I prefer to see things as they appear to be, reality being stimulating enough for my needs. When Maggie has drunk too much she turns with an O Christ of longing to whoever is nearest. The intensity of her desire to be liked causes her to weep upon unlikely shoulders. I do hope she conducted herself last night with sensibility as she lay in Edward's arms. The success of her plan to make him a legal if not natural father of her child depends on her avoidance of indulging in the truth. The fat and charming Billie may be her love, but an absent and unreliable one, and she can after all find solace for a long time in the overcrowded fields of her past memories. Besides, my knowledge of Maggie leads me to believe that she will transfer her love like a hat to another peg in the hall, for the Wild Colonial Boy to the chain-smoking geologist, without too much difficulty. Really looking at him now, sitting upright in the grass, engraved in sunlight, he is much to be envied. The qualities, imagined, that she will endow him with. Not now but later when her belly, unmarked, has yielded up its fruit, she will stand on some chair in some room and declare her love for him. The baby, the miniature Colonial Boy, chubby fists clenched with hunger, will gradually assume the features of the beloved and contented foster father. With a shrug the menopausal Maggie will disavow the seed that kindled him, and not until, if ever, a bowler sits upon the prematurely bald-ing head, will she recall her Billie Boy.

I did not envy Joseph his brief partnership. When I first wanted a bath in Morpeth Street Joseph had to be sent for to light the strong-willed geyser sagging on the wall. In an elegant flurry he struck the match and leapt backwards as the gas ignited. At the mild explosion his head twitched sharply. Maggie said that marriage had given him nervous habits. Separately at first then all at once, he would twitch, blink a holy brown eye and grind his teeth. Later when he increased in sophistication he wore a rubber band on his wrist and found comfort in pulling it clear of his flesh and letting it ping back with force. Maggie called him Father and God and Flower.

'Tell God the tea is made.'

'Tell Father to put Boy on the pottie.'

'Ask Flower to lend me ten shillings.'

That Maggie refused to change her laddered stockings or darn her ragged jumper filled him with distress.

A beautiful painting, he told me, whilst waiting for the geyser to explode, needs a decorative frame.

At our first meeting we nodded eagerly at each other and suffered misunderstandings. Neither of us was aware that we were equally and partially deaf until Maggie explained it.

'Norman prefers not to hear the cups and things rattling in the Kardomah,' she told him, 'so he lets the wax accumulate.' And to me, 'Joseph had a mastoid operation as a child which was a failure.' She looked thoughtfully and with admiration at his well-shaped ears. 'The surgeon was a friend of his father. They used to go climbing together in the Alps and they said it was so cold that the only time they felt warm was when they did a wee in their pants, and then it froze almost at once.'

'What?'

'That's what your father told me anyway.'

'Surely he never referred to it as wee?'

Shebah liked Joseph passionately, until, as she put it, money rotted him. I found him consistently charming and thought, as Maggie did, that he had married beneath him.

When I marry Jean I shall have married sensibly. Though politically I do not recognise class, my inner man rejoices at the limitations such a system imposes. To be respectable and yet roam at will beyond the barrier. To live wholly in Maggie's world would in the end defeat my aims. I derive enormous satisfaction from being a wolf in sheep's clothing. Bless the squire and his relations, keep us in our proper stations.

Up to a point last night my proper station would have been at the feet of Julia but for the talkative and restless Shebah. Having sung her song of divine forgiveness several times she sank into a high-backed chair almost in the centre of the room. Her feet stuck straight in front of her, she was completely hidden. Only one hand limpidly reproachful hung down over the arm of the chair. To Claud, facing her in a cane chair at the end of the room, she must have looked like Napoleon in exile on Elba, brooding over past victories. For me, behind her, she was a Zuleika of the river, parasol shading her face, trailing her scarlet fingers listlessly across the carpet, alone in a punt pulled by the current.

'What's up, old girl?' I shouted, kicking the back of her chair with my foot. No reply but an animal snarl and I rolled sideways to focus Claud and wink at him. He said something to her but I no longer cared to listen for, rolling back into position beneath Julia, I found my mouth conveniently close to her ankle, and laid my lips on it at once. She fidgeted but was frightened of moving her foot too brutally in case she kicked out my teeth. Taking advantage of her dilemma I caressed the plump calf of her leg and dug my fingers into the creased and damp bend of her knees. The pleasure I gained from pestering her in such a way was exquisite. Two little hands protestingly caught at my head and shook me.

'Don't,' she breathed. 'Please don't, Norman, dear.'

She was worried about Claud, but I was not. Having allowed me to stand naked and unadorned in his barn with his mistress without comment I felt it would have been surprising if he had suddenly objected to my chaste handling of her limbs.

'I do wish you wouldn't,' she whispered with spirit into my ears.

'Come downstairs with me,' I urged, sliding my hand across and above her polished and stockingless knees.

'No, I can't, really I can't.'

'Yes, you can. Come downstairs.'

'Norman dear, please don't, Claud will see you.'

With a sudden and delightful show of indignation she disengaged her foot and moved away from me. Lying on the floor I saw only her sensible shoes and her shapely legs. I almost, briefly, most briefly, felt like one of those men, unmet, who wear aprons and pay women to walk all over their tortured bodies. Then I suddenly imagined myself very tall, which is wishful thinking as I am extremely small, though in proportion. I cannot remember feeling tall before. Maybe it was a glimpse of Julia's feet going from me, that and the thought of those perverts of the apron world, giving me a false feeling of superiority and nobility. My feet are completely free from corns or blemishes.

Maggie, when dousing her feet in a bucket of water, constantly bemoaned her distorted and unsightly feet. Her father apparently had possessed arches like a ballet dancer's but failed to pass on their perfection.

The denseness of the carpet on which I lay was affecting my nasal passages. When I allowed my lids to close the room spun like a top. Opening them the pattern of the Persian floor covering slowed to a humdrum spiral of elaborate design, and I heard Claud saying ... 'You are so wise, my dear ... you accept it all.' With that my head jerked upright like a shuttle-cock, light at the top, and I jumped to my feet. I saw the back of Shebah's head and Claud staring up at her face as if she were his dearly beloved and before he could notice me I went down the stairs, under the angel everlastingly praying.

'Bless you, my darling angel,' I said, holding in my arms nothing. The obsessional hi-fi tones of the lately young. My darling, my angel. Unlike Claud I'm not fussy about my dream love. She doesn't have to be a Princess of the royal blood. Any woman will do. She laid her hot little cheek against my own as I went into the kitchen. I did hope Julia might be standing by the sink filling the kettle, but she wasn't. I watered the geranium on the sill and looked for bread in the cupboard. On the wall, above the empty hamster's cage, was a drawing done by Maggie in the days when she first met Claud. It is of herself, of course, staring out forever in the role of the child-woman, endlessly gazing with sensitivity at nothing in particular. I feel it would give Maggie consummate relief to say that she did not care about that one living there or that one dying there, and meaning it; just to move away without turning round lastly to see the ones she says she loves. The unbearable sadness of her supposed world, her private globe in which she lies impossibly mangled by unending imagined conflicts, turns her like water in a glass, the bubbles of her misery rising slowly to the surface and dissolving away.

I found a pen in the knife drawer and wrote 'Murphy was Here' on the edge of the drawing. I stood in the outer shop and visualised Billie edging his way between the tables and ornaments. Part of him must have been agreeably buoyant at coming to such an individualistic place.

'I have,' he told someone after the last butchering visit, 'been with friends in the country. He's an antique dealer, advises the museums from time to time, you know.'

With a diffident smile he purchased a stuffed mallard for thirty shillings and told Claud to keep the change. According to Claud, who may have been speaking less than the truth, he dropped it case and all in the yard when getting into his motor car. He left the glass all over the concrete. The exhaust smoke from the bottle green Crossley dropped like a veil and covered the shining pieces. Claud, to be even, directed him a good ten miles out of his route north, and kicked the glass into the flower beds, before taking Maggie out for a healing walk.

'She howled like a dog at each tree,' he told me.

'I was utterly mute all the way,' she told me.

Between the two it is safe to say that Maggie experienced a form of suffering. I am not sure what to think about her continual love pains. It is like when I try to explain to Jean what it means to me to climb mountains, hills though they be. My explanation is deliberately evasive because I do not intend her to understand, but I do offer such items as the air, its freshness that is, the view, very nice, the combined play of muscles, the convolutions of the mind, ah yes, particularly those, each item clear but external. I do not tell her of the fertile images my mountains bear. I do not even betray myself whilst telling her by the use of the possessive pronoun. But Maggie when she talks about her pain, her sadness, her desolation, shows no such reticence. They become in the end abstractions. That is why, when Maggie attempted to die, I experienced a shock out of all proportion to the deed. That she might do so was predictable, that she nearly accomplished it was incredible. There seemed to be a purity of intention that I had not comprehended in her.

The night before she went classically through the motions of betrayed girlhood. A delicate and crumpled crying before an audience of five grouped round the kitchen table. An attention to tea making, to being hospitable even though the world had disintegrated so dramatically about her ears such a short time ago. A careful cleansing of the teeth interrupted briefly whilst she uttered a moan of pain, followed by a girl guide utterance of obscenity. It was difficult to tell if the interlude was occasioned by her constantly sore gums or due to the traumatic homecoming of the Wild Colonial Boy. She said good night as charmingly and emptily as usual, performed the ritualistic round of handshaking that she affected, a habit instilled in her by her dead and homburg-hatted dad, gave her bargee laugh exposing all her large and now cleaned teeth, told me to make sure we were locked up for the night, and went to sleep in the bridal bed of polished brass.

When, the next morning, I rang, the predictable Maggie should have answered my persistent pronouncing of her name, a slurred tearful reply at most. Her silence, the emphatic drop of her telephone to the floor, caused a golden stream of melitose terror to run through my brain. Had I not phoned for Brenny to go to the house, had she not so conveniently met Arthur on the steps unlocking the front door, returning quite by chance for an application form for his driving licence, Maggie would have had the funeral we had so often talked about. All poppy wreaths and strong men reduced to tears and a tipsy vicar flinging himself into the freshly dug grave uttering cries of lamentation.

I have rationalised her actions in the only way of which I am capable. That she would have replied to my voice had she not drunk most of the contents of a bottle of gin left by Billie; that the alcohol had obliterated her very strong sense of social etiquette and liberated her stubbornness—hence her refusal to speak; that the gas she was inhaling had affected the muscles of her throat, had paralysed her organs of speech. Lastly, that her way of life had led her to a final pitch of absurdity and she had given way utterly to irresponsibility. The mother love she so often elaborates upon had evaporated like ether exposed to the air. Nothing remained of Maggie but poison in the blood stream, gas in the lungs and an immature mind impossibly seeking escape. She has told me she merely wished to sleep soundly for a few hours but I do not accept the explanation. Knowing her incapacity for drink she would have been sleeping long before the need to turn the tap of the cooker.

Whereas Maggie before this regrettable incident was a creature of light and shade, amusing and enchanting, harmless and without evil, she is now bracketed firmly in my mind as a hopeless neurotic, a feeble member of society, an enemy of the people. Feeling this I can still love her but no longer feel at ease with her. She has crossed the borderline ahead of me. I can watch from afar and marvel at her stupidity allied to an educated mind. Shebah is only Maggie taken to extremes of eccentricity forty years along. Her continued hold on her ovaries may in the end help her to survive but only comparatively. At least she will be spared hair on her curving upper lip. Without waxing so lyrical as Claud in his assertions that it is a privilege to live, it is a duty to live when there are children to be mothered. In due course should the unsuspecting Edward prove less than helpful, the local authorities may be called upon to remove the children into safe keeping. My harsh judgement, bearing in mind Shebah's edict that goodness should be suspected above all things, leads me to think that underneath I weep for golden girls all turned to dust. The face in the drawing on the wall in Claud's kitchen is not Maggie's face. It is only her conception of herself. Nothing more than a goose girl.

I almost ran back last night, like Dorian Grey, to see if the portrait oozed corruption, but instead I walked slowly upstairs again. Though air of paradise should fan the house and angels office all, nothing would in the end cause Shebah to cease her murmurings of hate. Loud and clear she abused the silent Claud, obscuring his face with her outflung war-like arms, so that I slipped through the room unseen and went into the bathroom where, washing her hands with lilac-scented soap, the molested Julia stood.

'I wondered where you were,' she said.

Her tone was friendly and her eyes were mild. Possibly she felt I could not commit an offence in a bathroom. As it happened I was no longer intending to do so. I was content to sit on the edge of the bath and have a conversation with her. Women will do strange things out of gratitude. They will even confide why they will not be seduced, forgetting that they pretended they did not understand the intention.

Maggie was always her most loquacious with me after having refused me the solace of her bed.

'There is something here,' she has said, 'which would positively ache if I were to be unfaithful.' Touching the region of her heart. There would follow a long and detailed discussion upon her current lover—his minute perversions, his vast inhibitions. They were all inhibited one way or another. Never having gained the citadel I cannot be sure if Maggie is equally repressed. To be frank it would have been impossible to find a time when Maggie would not be in a position of unfaithful-ness, her affairs came so thick and fast; thus she was spared a cardiac spasm induced by me. Any breathing space between lovers was in the nature of a few days, and those were taken up ritualistically with grief and melancholy and such statements as—

'Oh God, I'll never go through that again, Norman.'

'If you knew how it hurt . . . here.'

'I'll never feel the same again.'

'Why was he so strange . . . sick . . . odd . . . bitter?'

'I feel so sad. Honest to God I feel so sad, Norman.'

Oh, how her poor heart ached. It still causes distress that I never managed as it were to break into the magic circle and become the next tormentor. I was so suitably placed too, living only one floor up. One night she would be all sighings and lamentations, restless but quite resigned to a life of seclusion, and the next, when coming in for the alarm alock which was always kept in the food cupboard, she would be renascent with delight, all pluffy with hope and girlish giggles, head snapping back on her thin neck like a peony caught in a high wind, and saying: 'You see I met this man in the road, just by the railings of the Cathedral, armed with his rain-drenched hat, very nice with blue eyes and sort of lost looking. "Ho-ho," I said, "would you like to be a decoy? A real live automatic decoy with stuffed wings at the ready and beak all cleaned out?" And he said . . .'

It is still my belief that she will one day be the victim of a murderous assault. Once coming home late to the house in Morpeth Street I found the heavy front door ajar. The normal conclusion, the obvious one that somebody had not closed it after entering, did not occur to me. I took out my handkerchief and carefully wiped the curve of the brass knocker and the latch itself. In the dark hall I listened to the rapidity of my heart before turning the handle of Maggie's room. I switched on the light and used my handkerchief as a duster before looking at the brass bed. Maggie, alone, in the raincoat she sometimes wore as a nightgown, sat up alive and stared at me with sleep-laden eyes. 'Could you intend rape?' she asked me, reaching for the packet of cigarettes she always kept under the pillow. I told her about the open door and that I had expected to find her dead, arms held out in supplication, slivers of flesh scraped from her attacker's body wedged in the little fissures of her silver-tipped nails. She understood that my sympathies would naturally lie with her assassinator.

Just in case, we closed the heavy wooden shutters over the long window, shutting out the moon dipping like a toadstool into a glass of aniseed. I even bought a bolt and nailed it on the inside of her door but mostly she forgot to use it.

'Do you think, Norman,' asked the hair-combing Julia, 'that Claud looks better?'

She gazed at herself shortsightedly in the mirror above the hand basin.

'Oh yes, definitely, you've done wonders for him.'

It was after all the truth. She had held his whirling head to her breasts like a child and cuddled him to health. She had hidden the bottles of whisky and given him raw eggs in beakers to swallow. She had cleaned his living quarters and put the two hundred empty packets of cigarettes into the bin and listened to the noctural half words mumbled in the recurring nightmares. Maggie tried to describe what it was he went through but I found it ridiculous and irritating. All to do with hoof-beats thundering along the corridors of the brain, and an epiphany of someone, less than divine, rising monstrously in the mind, intent on destruction. Aaaah, goes he. Pit-a-pat of the heart which will be damaged beyond repair by the weight of the distraught mind's obsessional neurosis. Unless the nerve endings can be cauterised out of feeling, madness will follow from a haemorrhage of grief. Every thought doing a tittupy dance of self-annihilation, ungovernable. A cremation of the soul, a deglutination of the will. Let the sclerotic coating of the eyeball become cobwebby with tears.

I took this to mean that Claud was miserable because his wife had left him and was feeling guilty because he was to blame. I detest both obscurity and self-examination. I suspect these grief-stricken extroverts who tell their innermost thoughts to strangers on buses. Of course it was Maggie that told me this, not Claud, and she's not a stranger, and I don't think either of them would talk to a fellow bus traveller. Shebah is perfectly capable of doing so and in fact indulges quite frequently. But it's the way they analyse themselves so consciously and flagellate themselves with self-induced guilt. I do not experience guilt because I am ready to take the consequences of my own actions. I do not find myself in the ludicrous position of having to lay the blame for my illicit sex life at the breast of my mother who may or may not have denied me the nipples of her body. And if the school mistress who picked me off the playground asphalt when I was six years old, and massaged the agony of my bruised genitals, was less than wise, then at least I am in the end sensible enough to be grateful to her. Apart from the irritation which does not make negative the overall enjoyment, I derive much pleasure from the detailed confessions of these traumatic blatherers.

'You have no idea how sick he was when I first came here,' said Nurse Julia, studying her teeth for decay, 'vomiting every hour or so and dopey with pills and quite unable to sit still. Just went round and round like a dog to find somewhere to lie down and lick its sores.'

The image was an interesting one. In starched cap the gyral Julia followed the shaggy Claud round ever decreasing circles, until he fell on to his paws, only to start up again with an animal yelp of pain.

'And it was simply ages before he really slept at night. Months, you know. He kept seeing a ring she always wore on her finger.'

It is strange how they all fasten on to some article worn by the loved one. Claud and his wife's ring—Maggie and the check coat of the Wild Colonial Boy.

'Don't go,' Maggie had cried, two nights after she returned to Morpeth Street, following her illness. 'If you go the coat will come out of the walls at me.'

' "Don't let me sleep." ' Julia was speaking with the calmness of one who is no longer buffeted by storms but home and dry. ' "Don't let me go to sleep," he used to say. "If you do I'll see that damned ring." '

'How did you keep him awake?'

'I used to read him things, mostly from the Bible.'

I could well imagine. For a period Claud carried his Bible round like a talisman. He could give us a part but never the whole. We must however cleave to one another. It was a piece of advice that I could appreciate. I wondered how long it had taken Julia to cleave to him.

'Well, I shouldn't worry now,' I said, looking down at my feet on the cork bath mat, 'he's well on the mend. He looks as if he's thriving.' I was feeling sleepy. My head felt like lead; I wanted to go to sleep in the bath and, deep down, and it was quite a healthy emotion, I hated Claud. The whole house was littered with enemies of the people, traumatic blood suckers, indestructible and having all the fun. Maggie in bed with Edward—half dead a third of a year ago and now needing to eat enough for two—and Claud any time about to claim his mate and Bible thumping chum for the night. In fact I like Claud. I always have. Something about his matter-or-fact insanity that I find refreshing. I have during the last two years become almost an authority, in an amateur way, on eccentrics. And Claud is definitely man to man in his approach. One couldn't see him running berserk with a hypodermic syringe, like that doctor from Widnes who, lunging for Maggie's thigh, gave the photograph album an injection of behaviour liberating pethedine. His habit of crushing the bones of the hand when saying goodbye is more jocular than vicious. It will be interesting to note the exact degree of pain registered upon the smooth face of the departing Edward when Claud bids him farewell. I suppose his performance this morning with the air-rifle was a little more than good clean fun, but he did not shoot to kill. Had he mortally wounded Shebah I wonder where we should have buried the body.

Mrs Ryan in Morpeth Street had some relations who went on holiday to Spain with their mother-in-law, who died of old age suddenly in Andalusia. The formalities of burial were so complicated as to be impossible and she was put in a polythene bag on the top of the car for the sad journey home. As Mrs Ryan said: 'Them poor children asking for their grannie and she up on the roof under the boiling sun, like a chicken laid out by the heat.' Just near the frontier the family went a short walk only to find on their return that the car and Grannie had been stolen. Neither was ever recovered. It does not seem feasible to hope for such an occurrence in the peace of Hertfordshire. We could have put Shebah in the little plot under the trees, if only to benefit Claud's rose bushes. The tears that would have rolled down the cheeks of the mourning Maggie during the furtive burial service would have been no more indicative of despair than those of a child with gravelled knee. An episodal wound soon forgotten. Healing would be rapid and complete. 'Though the fault was mine, to forgive is divine,' Claud would hum softly in the summer nights of his careful pruning.

The light in the bathroom was very bright. Julia and I were

fully exposed and illuminated. Remembering the times Maggie has assured me that the reasons for women being unwilling are mainly visual and so obvious as to be generally overlooked by men—the mascara running down the kiss damp face, the soiled underwear, the cornfield stubble of shaven legs, the stretch lines on the stomach, the blackheads between the shoulder blades, the waxy ears, the pubic hair not copper rinsed or bleached, the feet with yellow soles—I stood suddenly upright and jerked the light cord down and released it and us into the gentle obliterating darkness. I was only going to attempt a mild and tender mingling of our mouths, a braille-like roving with my hands. I first removed her glasses and placed them with care on the shelf above the hand basin. I nuzzled her hair with my mouth and mumbled—'little darling, little dove'—into her hair. I had just unbuttoned the first two buttons of her blouse when the light was switched on again. I had not even managed to kiss her so busy had I been with my spectacle placing and my words of comfort. Maggie stood with the light cord in her hand, dressed in her cotton nightgown, and behind her Claud, not smiling, looking at the two buttons undone on the blouse of his mistress, and the tide of blood sweeping under the surface of her burning cheeks as she turned to grope for her spectacles.

He put his arm around Maggie and dipped his head into her neck, crooning ... 'O God, girl,' or something like that, as if he really cared. I was for a moment afraid I had overdone it, that this time he was angry, but Maggie looked at ease and she is a barometer of atmosphere. In her eyes there was nothing but curiosity and then Claud laughed into the warm skin of her shoulder. Then the two of them, Claud with lowered head and Julia with a faint agitation of her eyelids, went out of the bathroom and Maggie stayed at my back looking at her reflection in the mirror, lips curved in a Giaconda smile. We didn't speak because she was absorbed in being understanding and compatible with my mood. I did not have a mood to be compatible with and I would have liked to ask her about Edward, except she might have gone on too long and at too great a length, so I just whistled 'Devon, Glorious Devon'.

I'm not quite sure how much Maggie feels, despite her constant articulation. Sometimes I imagine if I could ask her quickly enough what she was thinking at a particular moment before she had time to marshal the words in force, she might answer ... nothing. A small round flat air-escaping negative. But I have never been swift enough. The words are all there, pyramid high and tumbling for exit. The shapes they make build up in her emotional structures. I am unhappy she will say, and like Pavlov's dog when the bell rang, the saliva of her suffering begins to dribble.

In the living room Shebah was still singing. She stared at Maggie as if she had newly risen from the dead, mouth wide open on a high note of shrill surprise. I was not feeling very cheerful. Twice in one night I had been cruelly interrupted in the pursuit of the angel-protected Julia. Altogether the sort of evening that, had I been on home ground, I would have terminated by winding up the alarm clock and going upstairs. I felt, however, that something might yet happen, though not in any spectacular sense, in that overcrowded room, as long as Claud still ran round and round cracking his invisible whip. He lit a cigarette for the debauched Maggie sitting like a pink Buddha in the huge armchair, and poured more wine without her knowledge into the glass that the gesticulating Shebah held aloft like a flower she might yet toss to her forgiving lover. It was surprising that Shebah had not by now heeled over unconscious, unless canny to the last she had been decanting the drink into the many pots and vases about the room. Claud was standing in front of me, touching his breast bone through the open front of his shirt, the fingers playing a slow scale of notes across the hairless skin. Whilst I looked at him, try as I might, like a tired man nodding towards sleep, I kept sliding off the glittering arc of his eyeballs. Each time he moved his head I was flung outwards and everything in the room was shiny and moving with moist light and there were a series of snapshots— a girl in a nightgown of silly pink, an old woman waving her arms in anguish, a dog with its head on its freckled paws—and Claud was talking:

'... quite impossible to tell how much is already there to be released, cocker. We all have our postures you know. I reckon you've got a pretty solid posture.'

He waggled the bowl of his glass under my nose as if he intended to grind it into splinters up my nostrils. Julia appeared a little to my left with pale combed hair and Shebah, chest puffed out with billowy scarves, flew like an owl towards her.

'The only thing to do man is to become part of the cosmic flow. Spin like a dervish and never bother to find out what it's about. At my age there's no time left for conjecture....'

There was much more but I was trying to reason out what Claud's exact age was and whether he looked it, and seeing him twenty years ago in air-force blue, dapper and bonny with beardless chin and the plum mouth unprotected, and how long I could keep my hair combed forward so as to minimise its thinness, without being affected and running the risk of a chill breeze lifting it clear and exposing the waxy dome. I take great care with my diet and with all the getting up my mountains, not to mention my more erotic exercises. I should stay slender for another thirty years. But I do worry about my hair. It's all right for the Wild Colonial Boy to sport his weathered bald crown. His particular height and porky-boy belly put him into a defined category. As Maggie has told me, there is something extremely attractive about the man running rapidly to seed. Like a cabbage grown purple and out of all proportion the mind is filled with sinful thoughts. But the small man, me, the precise man, must take care not to degenerate into an elderly whippet running like hell with emaciated flanks after the mechanical rabbit in the Waterloo Cup. There and then I decided to abandon my flat cap, and was aware of Claud still talking ...

'... advertisements, television commercials, everything bent on the image of the uplifted breast beneath the clinging sweater. Not a nipple in sight that's meant for lactation, only for the visual stimulation of the male. Too much erotic sex, too much mental titillation, leaving the common man unfit for reality copulation, only fit for woosome twosome masturbation. The fantasy life that goes on is simply incredible. A million commuters in bowler hats avidly chasing fat women and Lolitas between jumping lines of their evening newspapers. A million breasty girls utterly unaware that babies must be fed naturally, not handed the bottle every four hours....' His mouth opened and shut as the words buzzed like wasps through his jammy lips. The ball of wool that was his beard climbed up his cheeks and thrust strands into the craters of his ears.

'... but she was different. Now she was a woman.' Who was he alluding to now? Surely not Maggie with her lemon shaped breasts trapped within her safety-pinned brassière.

'... there was real glory, man. Real glory.'

With a final collision of her percussion lips the last notes of his orchestral work vibrated to a close. A fleck of dew was flung trembling from the flat leaf of his tongue. With a warm smile the maestro glanced across at Maggie who fondly returned his look until Shebah blacked out their view with her dark-garbed body.

'A remarkable woman,' said Claud. Shebah or Maggie? I presumed Shebah.

'The Jews are a very *sympatico* race you know, cocker.' He was taking me by the arm and not so much leading as pushing me towards his bedroom. The fingers round my upper arm were like steel, the voice flowed on endlessly—

'Generations of persecution have given wings to their sensitivity. If you blind the nightingale the song will be sweeter. It is the nature. All life is a circle and the end of all our beginnings is to arrive where we started and to know the place for the first time.' He opened the bedroom door and thrust me inside.

Quite so. I did not know the place nor had I at any time. I looked intently at the elegant bed, the shell pink walls, the bitter glimpse of Julia's nightdress half showing beneath a cushion, whilst Claud undid his shoes. His articulation continued, spattered by grunts as he struggled with his socks. 'Nothing you do will in the end appease the monster that lies in wait for you. For every crime there is a punishment. Every hurt given, every lie told, every atom of suffering deposited by you on the surface of another human being will bring its awful reward. Neither money, nor power, nor threats, nor pleadings will avail you.'

He sank on the bed thrusting out his naked feet and lit a cigarette, puffing at it energetically, brows deeply furrowed, like a girl concentrating on blowing away the seedling head of a dandelion—he loves me, he loves me not—until behind a cloud of smoke he asked abruptly and looking at a point on the wall above my head, 'Did Julia seem to like it?'

'Well, yes and no. More polite than anything, I think.'

I watched his big toes paddling in the quilted coverlet and hoped I was hitting the right conversational note. He put his cigarette down on the edge of the bedside table and began to lift his shirt up from the waistband of his trousers. Was he going to bed or about to perform some naked dance? Was he

111

perhaps trying to show me that he too was adept at removing his clothes with speed? If so he was less than convincing. He took at least half a minute to get the shirt over his head and emerge with scarlet face and disordered beard. 'I don't mind,' he said, rising to his feet and drawing in his stomach. 'That is to say I mind very much, or would if I could. But the heart's died on me, man. I am but a shell that once lay near the sea. I imagine I hear the sound of it yet, but it's all a dream.'

He looked thoughtfully at his feet and slapped with one hand at his huge diaphragm. The drink had larded him with fat but he was still impressive. The skin shone perfectly smooth and without blemish. 'I am going to attend to my roses,' he informed the pink wall, and reached for his dressing gown that hung behind the door. He seemed undecided what to do further once the cord round his waist was tied. He put one arm inside the pouch of his gown and began to pace, Nelson-wise, across the room.

'Of course she's devoted to me...' he paused and rubbed at his hidden armpit. Surely there was hair there? It seemed strange that his face and head were so overgrown. A little pit of ginger warmth where the honey sweat trickled free.

'... utterly loyal.... If it's loyalty one wants?' He gazed at me as if I had a problem.

'I know, I know what you mean,' I said emphatically, nodding my head vigorously like some bidder at an auction sale. I had no idea what he meant but he seemed in need of affirmation.

'Of course I don't believe a word Shebah says,' he went on, striding past me to the window. 'It's all in her mind and even if it were true it doesn't change things any.' As he turned to continue with his self-imposed sentry duty the light caught his face and reflected moisture on the surface of his eyes. It may have been caused by the smoke from his cigarette and it may have been tears. If so they were unshed and blinked clear before I could be certain, and he moved very quickly and seized me by the lapels of my jacket.

'Now look here, mate,' he shouted, transforming himself into the bully at large, fiercely keeping his eyes on mine, 'keep your hands off my woman. I won't stand for it, do you hear?'

The little broken veins under the surface of his hair-strewn cheeks were suddenly engorged with the surge of anger that stained his face scarlet. He trembled with indignation, head thrust back like an illustration of an actor in one of Shebah's out-dated theatre books, face registering rage with nobility, pouty mouth firmly closed, blue eyes round as buttons, hard and unrelenting. Before I had time to respond in any way myself—I was just about to contort my facial muscles into a portrayal of fear with cunning—he released me and said quite calmly: 'Study the humble bee, cocker. The order of their life is beyond belief.'

He adjusted his dressing gown and went like a Japanese warrior out of the room towards the fragrance of his roses. Alone and unmolested I flattened my hair smooth with my hand and eased my jacket back into shape. The way in which clothes hang on a man can be indicative of character. Though not as orderly as the humble bee, I am neat. Outside the window a curve of main road lit by lamps and some new houses built like boxes with low brick walls, was not unlike the street I will finally settle in when Jean and I are married. There was a light burning in the upstairs room and I peered closely to see a human figure removing its garments. The glass was cold against my nose and I could see no one. The structure of the Hive, as Claud could doubtless tell me, is based on a geometric principle. Everything within is precise and fragrant. In the garden of the house opposite a plaster gnome stood under a bush clutching a plaster spade. I warmed my nose with my hand and considered it safe to return to the living room.

It was empty of Claud and Maggie and Julia. Only Shebah, enthroned in her papal chair, sat facing the far wall, arm outflung. I sat down behind her and watched the white fat wrist circled with its handcuff bracelets twist back and forth above the carpet. After a little while with a great deal of shuffling and groaning she began to slew the chair round to face me. In spite of her constant references to her delicate state of health she has the strength of a man. As if driving a difficult and outmoded automobile she manoeuvred her vehicle to a halt and, breathing heavily, stared at me with passion. The black beret she always wears was askew on her grey head; a smear of lipstick lay petal-shaped across the powdery chin. My affection for her, though not often manifested, is real. She shares my disillusionment with Maggie. She has in a different way from me been deprived of her just rewards. She was forced to her chagrin to play the buffoon for Maggie's Friday night carnivals. Whilst I was kept from physical union, Shebah was frustrated in her attempts at full communion. Echoing Claud's statement, Maggie gave a part but never the whole. Endlessly restless and unfulfilled the tortured Israelite jiggled her bottom in the upholstered chair and swung her trembling calves. I began in my mind to dissolve the fat around her hips and waist, to draw back the folds of the ruined face, stain each blade of hair with black, and give back lustre to the eyes. The disguise penetrated, the Gaiety girl of forty years ago stirred and fixed me with a look of insolent disdain. The bossy maiden arched her brows and declined to go into the garden with me. Tossing back the blue mantle of her hair, the Ilse Koch of Morpeth Street slaps at her plastic galoshes with a rawhide whip. Anti-semitic to the bone she clears the synagogue of money lenders and finds herself alone for Yom Kippur.

'A misunderstanding,' she cried. 'Always I have been mis-understood.' With a sea-wave curl of her upper lip, heavy with crimson dye, she transforms her friends, in a misunderstood way, into mortal enemies. Running from one end of her life to the other she asks the same unanswered question—'Why me? ... Why me?'

If she can be believed, and why not, she has hinted at affairs of frantic love. Whether they were consummated she has not divulged. What outrageous admirer prised wide her clever thighs and perpetrated love? The gulf between her notion of an affair and mine is like the sun from the earth ninety-three million miles distant, and yet it appears it is she who has been consumed by fire.

As her eyes were telling me across the flower-strewn carpet last night—What do you know, darling? As if to underline her contempt for my ignorance of life she raised one bangled arm wearily and fluttered her scarlet-tipped fingers. A graceful movement. That is why later when she stumbled against Claud's china cabinet, shattering the glass a little and jostling the ornaments within, I felt such surprise. Because she is not clumsy; her gestures, even those of contempt, are always de-fined.

I had gone downstairs to find Julia and met Maggie and held her in my arms, whilst she enacted one of her loving friend's scenes for the benefit of Edward, who had materialised out of nowhere and stood at the top of the stairs, his black hair ruffled from slumber, almost cross but finally relenting and leading her back to the nuptial chamber. Julia, ever busy in her protection of Claud's property, crouched down behind the sofa and began to clean the harp which lay on its side. She gave me a little rag dipped in paraffin with which to wipe the strings, and secure in the knowledge that I was doing a useful job I lay down beside her on the floor. Claud, bare to the waist, sat on a piano stool and closed his vigilant eyes. I could hear the voice of Shebah rise and fall in a cadence of sound and once I heard Claud say—'Yes, my dear, you may be right'—in reply to some comment she had made. Behind the sofa, immersed in my restorative labour, all was peace and calm, a little oasis of shade in the hectic furnished room.

In the old days at Morpeth Street we would all by now be sickly clinging to our pillows; Maggie's at least, if not Claud's, would be damp with tears.

Maybe it is the difference between town and country, between the windows flung wide to the summer night and the broken panes in the frames nailed fast for fear of thieves. On all the beds here clean sheets and in the kitchen the supper dishes washed and in the garden the roses free from parasites. Maybe the difference is in the atmosphere created by the sane and tidy Julia. I no longer wanted to caress her, or to anger my seated host with the face of repose, nor did I particularly want to clean his harp, but I was a guest and my bed was to be the sofa behind which I lay and I was too inhibited by upbringing to retire there and then. So I continued to rub, rub, rub, with my little rag up and down the silver strings, pleasantly aware of the smell of Julia's hair without being disturbed by it, and thought of Jean, a little, and Maggie, a lot, and myself most of all. The danger of being on intimate terms with such people lies in the inevitability with which sooner or later, however environmentally opposed to their mode of thinking, one is contaminated sufficiently to start the sickening process of self-analysis. I did indulge in an analysis in the days when I lived at home, but then I liked myself more. Though I am not naturally honest I have been so by chance. I was mainly thinking about the time Maggie and I had decided to obtain some stained glass from the partially demolished church near to the house. Maggie had some idea, never executed, that she would make a big framed panel and place it in the back yard. Years ago when she was very young and had been going to visit Joseph in the studio he had in the next street, she had sat

in the then resplendent church in order not to seem too eager
and to keep him waiting. 'It will be a kind of memorial,' she
told me, 'to Joseph and the past, and it will be a perfect foil for
the sunflowers.'

The half-caste boy next door, borstal educated, had told us
about the glass. 'That coloured bastard me dad,' he said,
jerking an eloquent thumb in the direction of his limping
parent, 'seen it lying about all over the place.'

When we found the church the only window intact was high
up on the southern wall, encased in lead and anchored in
cement, but I knelt down and Maggie climbed upon my shoulders and I straightened myself very carefully and she lunged
forward with her Woolworth's hammer. There was a dull thud
and then a high shivering vibration which was too real to be
just in my mind, and at first I thought I had plucked one of the
harp strings by mistake, and sat there bemused with the rag in
my hand, till Julia knelt upright so that her head was above the
level of the sofa and said in a tone very chill but still lady-like:
'Oh Christ.'

When I looked over the top of the sofa back with my arms
dangling like some surf-rider breasting a large and embroidered
wave, Shebah was huddled against the wall, hands to her face,
and Claud still on his stool staring at her with wide open eyes.
A clock chimed in the shop below.

'How's it going, man?' asked Claud, apparently of me
though he did not look in my direction.

'Fine, fine,' I replied, distracted somewhat by the little
moans of distress issuing from the cowering Shebah.

She moved suddenly as if propelled by an almighty hand and
touched the case of china figures. I thought she was in one of
her appreciation of beauty moods, a little accentuated by drink,
her pigtail sticking straight out under the black beret, her
whole body writhing against the cabinet. How often has she
cried to be given patience to endure her load, she with the soul
made for loveliness. It appeared to me that she had thrown
patience aside and was about to seize her rightful portion, and
she might have done had not Claud cried out—'Leave it,
Shebah'—very stern, as if he was addressing the dog, and on
that too harsh note of command Julia ran forward and cradled
the desperate art-lover in her arms and led her to the sofa. In a
spastic fit of lamentation Shebah tossed her ruined head and
jerked the spectacles from the nose of Julia.

'O, darling, I'm so sorry.'

The penitent fumbled with her near blind comforter in an effort to restore sight. Claud came to inspect the half-cleaned harp and patted me on the shoulder—'Well done, man'—and rubbed his chest, leaving a smear of grease. Rough winds continuing to shake the darling buds of May, in this case Julia's breasts on whose swellings Shebah continued to roll, I sank down into my little world inhabited by a harp, a yard of carpet and a shadow cast by the golden lamp on the piano.

I felt that the evening's entertainment was almost over, that the manly Claud was about to take down the tent. He began moving wine glasses and bottles on to a tray and presently the broken Shebah made her round of weepy good nights. She who had been wont to cry out—'But Life is Sweet, my children'—more because she liked the poetry of it than because she believed in the sentiment, now stumbled on white sandalled feet out of the room, evidently convinced that life was vile. One of her scarves, like Salome's veil, caught on the door and drifted from her bowed shoulders to the floor. Julia brought blankets from the bedroom and made up my bed on the sofa, like the good little woman she is, smoothing my sheets and plumping up my pillow. They left me, Claud with many instructions about switching off the lights and securing the window, and Julia with a sweet smile playing upon her pale exhausted lips.

'Sleep well, Norman dear,' she said without malice, patting the flank of the brown dog that lay asleep on the floor.

I took off my clothes and shoes and waited on the sofa. I folded my hands in my lap and felt like an adolescent girl, except that my feet were impossibly large, and the hands that hid the one thing that prevented me being a blonde maid were dusted across the knuckles with sandy hairs.

When I heard the sound of bedsprings jangling in the outer bedroom—Claud's own particular brand of psychological torture, meant especially for me—I went to the china cabinet and eased open the door. Inside there was a white dog with a coloured snout lying on its side, and a little porcelain box decorated with flowers that was in two pieces and a pair of figures that seemed untouched. One was of a girl in dress and cap leaning her elbow on a bird-cage stand, head hung low, fist bunched against her mouth, and one hand held towards me with a lolling little bird on her open palm. The companion figure was a pretty man in knee-breeches with a dimpled face, who leaned on a spade. He was supported at the buttocks by a tree trunk twined about with ivy. I took one in each hand and carried them to the light. As far as I could see they were perfectly intact. In my palms they lay pale as milk. My thighs in the lamplight looked yellow and thick. The elasticated top of my socks had printed a pink ridge across my calves. I tried dropping one of the figures on the floor, but it rolled harmlessly upon the carpet. The dog, asleep, twitched its silken ears. I picked up the little manikin and took him and his companion into the bathroom. I laid a towel across the cork bath mat and, turning the taps in the hand basin full on, knelt down and struck the two figures one against the other. The hand holding the limp bird broke at the wrist and rolled under the bath. A button had gone from the bodice of the girl and two knuckles from the spade-clasping hand of the gallant grave digger lay in chippings on the towel. I searched for the missing button for a moment and then thought how much better it would be if Claud, some time searching for the dropped top of his toothpaste tube, came upon it unawares. I took the spoiled figures and the pieces back into the main room and replaced them on the shelves inside the cabinet. The dog during my absence had climbed on to the sofa and lay with its tail on my pillow. When the lamps were extinguished there was a rind of dawn light outside the closed windows. The springs of Claud's bed trembled in a final cadenza.

This morning Claud brought me a cup of tea. When he opened the windows birds sang and sunlight glinted on splinters of glass on the carpet. He went downstairs and came back with a brush and swept the floor, a tuft of beard clenched between his teeth. He did not look in the cabinet at all and when he came to fetch my empty cup he smelled of scented soap and toothpaste, and on the surface of his pink and fleshy chest, revealed by his open dressing gown, there were two marks faintly scored. Scratch marks of fingernails. Not his.

In the bathroom I looked again for the missing button from the dress of the china girl but I was unlucky, there being nothing but dust and a hairgrip belonging to Julia presumably. I put the clip in the pocket of my jacket without any real reason. I'm not in love with Julia. Shebah tried to turn the handle of the locked door and swore and moved away sighing heavily. I cannot imagine that she wanted to wash, only that she wished to pass water. It may be that she urinated with fright when ten minutes later the pellet hit her in the ankle. I do not know why I harbour at times such intense feelings of antagonism against her and Maggie. Though not an ordinary girl, lying there in a patch of sun, morose bottom lip quivering over some secret thought, Maggie is still deserving more of compassion than hatred. My ambiguity distresses me, being at the root emotional, and I do not care for emotions. I do not detest my parents for their futile adherence to the conventions, their blind belief in the dignity of human toil, their comical loyalty to the Royal Family. I do, it is true, take some measure of delight in puzzling my workmates at the factory by a deliberate show of eccentricity, but there is no malice intended. I do not either, as Maggie does, suffer from being related to my mother and father. Should my own father, as hers did, confide to me one tea-time, that life was a cheat and a delusion, I would agree with him without identifying myself personally with his statement; nor would I feel the weight of seventy wasted years. Nor do I expend energy on uselessly worrying about whether I am understood. It is not necessary to be understood in order to live. I am aware that my parents, like the vast majority of the English working class, are ignorant and childish. Under a different system they would be educated sufficiently to be neither childlike-pattern repeating nor ignorant-uninformed. Maggie and Shebah, not being childish or ignorant, I am forced to the conclusion that possibly education alone is not enough. Believing as I do in Marxist ideology and yet actively participating in the survival of capitalism puts me in much the same dilemma as Shebah. The martyr without a cause. I am cut off from fulfilment. But I do not sympathise with Shebah, recognising that she is dangerous and to be discouraged. The kindness she has received from Julia and Maggie following her breakages last night, and her wound this morning, have sunk her in a coma of satisfaction, sitting in her white cane chair, sugary and quiet. Having obtained such a liberal injection of pity she may well demand another and larger dose before long. Fortunately I do not have to travel on the train with her. Some other luckless traveller will find her mock swooning across the carriage seats, clutching her leg as if the marrow had run out. Even Claud at lunch time gave her more than the rest of us.

'Get that down you, my dear.'

'Oh, darling, I couldn't.'

'No arguments. Eat up. Make a new woman of you.'

'Oh, darling.'

The new woman opened her carmined mouth and ate all that was on her plate; little dribbles of masticating laughter came from the corners of her lips.

Maggie has been almost silent since breakfast. She has held the hand of the placid Edward as if afraid he might yet make a break for it. He has played with the children and thrown sticks for the dogs and behaved like a gentleman, which he possibly is. We will have to wait the few long weeks till Maggie tells him the glad tidings of his approaching fatherhood. 'Of course I cannot be sure,' she will say, holding her breath to keep her belly flat, 'but it's almost definite.'

Maggie and I arranged some time ago that we would meet in the Kardomah in extreme old age to discuss the outcome of our lives. Shebah, long since buried, will achieve resurrection through memories over the cups of coffee held between tremulous fingers. From her island retreat off the coast of Scotland, stockinged folkweave fashion in homespun wool of darkest green, Maggie, if not grown bald, will shake her white fringed head and lay a wrinkled paw upon my bony knee.

'Now tell me, Norman, do tell me, Flower, what happened all those years ago that night at Claud's?'

Maybe I shall only remember the sunshine in the garden and the strip of bandage round the ankle of Shebah, her comic flag of truce, and the ham we had for lunch lying on a bed of lettuce leaves. Then we shall recall no doubt with awe Shebah's heroic tolerance of cold and rain, the insatiability of her curious mind grubbing for truths in books grown mildewed. I shall long since have read nothing save the columns of the lately dead and the newly born, like my father before me, in the local evening newspaper, seated in my chair by the fire in my little mortgaged box with the neat clippered hedges outside. My mouth, corseted by teeth not my own, will fill with spittle, a reservoir of juice shallow as the microscopic follies of my youth, which I shall swallow and regurgitate anew, till the dates and names of my little life finally dry into a hard crust at the corners of my fallen lips.

Nothing to remember about this weekend at all. Someone perhaps found a daddy to rock the baby's cradle and bestow on it a surname to round off the Christian name of William, and someone perhaps found extreme pleasure in the minute wound in the flesh of a swollen ankle. But I cannot be sure I shall remember, being so uninvolved.

Maggie has just stretched out a loving hand to the quiet Edward. She smiles, a fantasy smile in the afternoon garden.

'Gentlemen of the Jury, I ask you, how much more proof do you require of this woman's duplicity? You have heard the evidence against her, you have been aware of the many witnesses called in her defence, a vast swaggering line of improbable human beings, apart from the gentleman in the Victorian collar. He at least, though refusing to take the Biblical oath, has not lied.' The sunlight pours through the window, cathedral rays about the head of the one and only beatnik landlady as she raises angelic eyes in the direction of the judge. A moment of indecision, a pause for reflection, then ... 'Case dismissed.' And with the dismissal a roar of triumph from Claud rising to his feet with outstretched arms, a groan from Shebah, an audible sigh as the professor slumps forward unconscious and seconds later in the corridor beyond, Maggie, vindicated, tweaking—because Havelock Ellis says it's permissible—the nipples of the judge. His wig falls from his rocking balding head ... 'Please,' he supplicates, 'let me come and visit you.'

'Of course. Tea next Friday. Only a little intimate group.'

Quite so. As Baudelaire tells us ... Nothing that is not misunderstanding. Claud in his frock coat helps us all into the yellow car. Miss Charters, shuffling endlessly in the peel-strewn gutters, lifts eyes filled with momentary recognition ... 'Ah your daddy goes to sea' ... Like a round of applause the sky cracks and rain pours down. From somewhere a voice begins to sing what Maggie calls 'our song' ...

> *'I wandered today by the hills, Maggie,*
> *Where you and I were young ...'*

The mind if it ceased from boggling could multiply the fantasies without end.

If one was involved.

If one cared.

'What did you say he was called?' asked Betty.

'What?' For a moment Julia's eyes behind her spectacles were devoid of expression. She looked at Betty and did not see her.

'Oh, Norman. You mean what Maggie calls him?'

'Yes. The name Maggie calls him.'

With the use of the name Betty felt the unknown woman was suddenly in the room.

'Edwardian Norman, wasn't it?'

Claud gave a lusty laugh of short duration and removed his arm from Betty's shoulders. She felt cold and unprotected almost at once.

'Wrong period, my dear. Victorian Norman.'

He got up and moved about the room without much purpose. He passed Stanley twice and each time gave him a half smile to which the man responded with embarrassment.

'Why are they all friends?' asked Betty. She felt she was putting too many questions but suddenly she did want to know. She noted that Stanley at the other side of the room was looking at her with surprise. It occurred to her that his face was like a blank sheet of paper, crumpled with no message to be read. 'I mean,' she continued, 'they're so different. All of them. Maggie and Norman and the old woman.' It was extraordinary how familiar they became when she named them like that.

'Yes, they are different.' Julia still sat with the photograph in the palm of her hand. 'I suppose they are very different, but they all seem alike when they're together. Claud seems like them too when they're together.' A frown creased her smooth forehead. 'I'm not like them at all.'

'No you're not. You're not like them, are you, girl?' Claud stood beside her, not touching her, but looking down at her. 'You're my own dear girl, my very dear girl, that's what you are.'

A tide of scarlet pleasure suffused her face; even the tips of her small ears glowed. Claud thought to himself that it was the truth. His own dear girl, the girl that was dear to him. Someone to whom he belonged and who belonged to him. At least it was the truth this moment in time whilst he felt it. He had written to Maggie only a week ago and told her to seek what he had found. They had not met for months though they had telephone conversations.

'How is it, my love?'

'Not too bad, my love.'

'Can't you come here, my love, with the children and get strong?'

'How can I, love? I can't keep wandering about like a lost tribe. They've missed so much school already.'

'It's so peaceful here, my love. Julia doing the ironing and the baby asleep in its cot. Not great glory, my love, but beautiful. Can't you come?'

'No, I can't. I don't really know what to do. The man from the National Assistance didn't come.'

'Didn't he, darling?'

'No. I was all ready you know in needy sort of clothes and the new iron hidden in the cupboard and he just didn't come.'

'Shall I send you some money, my love?'

'No. I don't want any money really. I just want something. Honest to God I just want something.'

'I reckon you do, my love. Can't you find some good old boy, simple and uncomplicated? Can't you, darling?'

'Oh, you and your hairy roadsweepers. I don't know any good old boys or simple farm hands or carpenters . . .'

And a lot more about the latest lover who had been going to be the last and how now he wouldn't be after all because he didn't really love her. Of course he still said he loved her but she knew he didn't. She always knew that. Then the tears unlinking in her throat making her voice not quite steady and a long pause and then . . .'

'I must go, love, the phone bill will be awful.'

'All right, my love. I'll write you a letter.'

'Yes, do that.'

'Good night, my dear love.'

'Good night, Claud. Take care.'

And at the other end of the line a click as the phone was replaced and an image of Maggie in her flat, at her desk, with wet cheeks and her hand held to her mouth, touching her lips that are trembling, and her other hand, the one with the silver ring, searching for cigarettes.

He was not too worried about her, though she was too restrained, he felt. In the old days when he had phoned her twice daily and sometimes in the middle of the night, when he was sick, he had howled down the phone like some animal in pain. Perhaps it was the drink that had helped him not to care what he said, what words he chose. Behind Maggie's conversations were the unsaid sentences, held back, which he knew about, the words that would let loose the grief, and as she told him, how could she do that when she had to take the children to school in the morning, and she had to keep calm? He comforted himself by thinking that soon there would be someone else to absorb her attention and give her happiness, even if only for a while. Not the long endless contentment he was to know with Julia and his new children, but something.

Stanley said: 'Look here, Mr White, we really must go. We've taken up so much of your time already and I have to go to the office this afternoon.'

'What's your line of business, man?' As if passionately interested Claud stood before him and waited.

'Oh, I'm in advertising actually. Not very interesting I'm afraid, but I do quite well.' He seemed almost to be apologising for his calling in life, his manner of earning his daily bread and paying for antique desks. 'It was my father's business originally, in a much smaller way of course in his day and I've expanded it a lot, you know.'

Betty was uncomfortable listening to her husband, watching his scrap of a mouth opening and closing, saying a lot of unimportant things. It wasn't that she was ashamed of him, it was more that she felt they were wasting time, that in this room or any other room that this man with the beard happened to be in, there was something she could learn. She said quickly: 'Was your father an antique dealer, Mr White?'

'Good God no. Nothing like that.' He gave vent to another burst of laughter. 'Good that, eh, Julia?' Julia was looking at the photograph again; unwillingly she gave her attention to Claud.

'What, dear?'

'They want to know if my old man was in the antique line. Wanted to know if he was a dealer.' Again he laughed. His lips opened to show his teeth and the tip of his small pointed tongue. 'Good that,' he repeated. 'A dealer. More of a sadist I reckon.' He turned to Stanley and looked at the knot of his tie. 'My father was a very hard man. Took great pleasure in beating the daylights out of me every moment he could spare. A dealer in punishment. I was afraid of him all my life, all my childish life that is. Now I just dislike him.' He hoped he was not sounding too obvious. In the last few years he had realised he was becoming obvious. The way the woman Betty was looking at him he thought it would not matter how obvious he became, but about Stanley he was not so sure. 'All our problems now, our mismanaged lives, point backwards to our childhood experiences.' He saw that he was amusing Stanley or embarrassing him; the beginnings of a smile drifted across the man's face, but Claud forced himself to continue: 'Take Maggie, for instance. When she complains that this one or that one doesn't really love her, what is she really saying, eh? What's she really saying?'

Betty felt terrible. He was looking straight at her and she could not think how to answer. She didn't even know what the question was. She moistened her lips and thankfully heard Claud say: 'She's saying "they" didn't love her. She's saying her parents never loved her, she's saying no one ever loved her because they never could. She's saying if they didn't love her then nobody else can, and she's saying she doesn't want anyone else to love her.'

In the silence Stanley said mildly, 'I got on very well with my old man.' He said it deliberately. He hadn't in actual fact but he saw no reason to bare his innermost soul just for the hell of it. The man was so damned self-indulgent and so damned feminine and Betty was simply making a fool of herself. He looked at his wife sitting on the sofa beside Julia, her eyes fixed on the antique dealer.

'Victorian Norman,' said Julia, 'had a perfectly normal childhood. He told me so. He was very happy. How do you explain him?'

'Ah, well,' Claud said, 'he's just intelligent. He's a perfectly adjusted but intelligent human being. He can have the best of both worlds. And he's well adjusted because he had a happy childhood.'

'Yes, but he's not normal,' insisted Julia.

'That's because he's intelligent.'

'Oh, come now,' said Stanley, 'surely you don't claim that anyone who is intelligent is not normal?'

'I do, I do, man. It's impossible to be normal and intelligent. Intelligence is merely the definition of the faculty to be able to reason. And the man who can reason all this mess out, this chaos, can't be normal. Where is the life we have lost in living, eh? Where have all the flowers gone? Where are the Earls of Bushy, Bagot and Green?'

Stanley laughed openly at this. He found Claud very charming. The man talked such nonsense with such authority, but Betty's face was serious.

'Is Maggie very intelligent?'

'Not really. She's just a woman. Women have a way of understanding most things. Do you know what Gertrude Stein said when she was dying, girl?'

Betty did not even know who Gertrude Stein was. She wasn't on the photograph at any rate. She said in a small voice: 'No, what did she say?'

'She said "What is the Answer?" And when no one replied she said "What is the Question?" How's that, eh, girl, how's that?'

'Did she really say that,' asked Julia, 'did she really, Claud?'

'Yes, really, my love. That and "A rose is a rose is a rose".'

'It sounds like Shebah,' said Julia.

'We really must go now, Betty.' Stanley came over to the sofa and held out his hand to his wife. 'Come on.'

She ignored his outstretched arm and looked at the photograph on Julia's knee. The old woman with the bandage round her leg sat on her cane chair. Her eyes were veiled by the thick lenses of her curious glasses. A rose is a rose is a rose, thought Betty, a rose is a rose is a rose. . . .

Shebah

If there is any sense in this, it eludes me. I find myself, almost, yes almost, carried along by their general attitude of abandonment. They do it all with such an air, with such an absence of shame, with such complacency.

Was there even a feeling of reality in the way they picked me up off the ground this morning?

Do I, as Maggie would have it, inhabit another sphere of existence altogether?

Sitting here in a garden, not alone for once (surrounded by scum), really very weary. I wish Maggie would not keep throwing me those wan little smiles. I cannot bear her massive insincerity. Like this morning: not one of them daring to say a word to that swine Claud. Here in all this luxury to be shot at like an animal, hunted through the grass like some exalted form of game. It is unbelievable and yet quite comprehensible.

Did I not run down Brownlow Hill, poor little me with my violin case under my arm, and all the gentile children calling after me . . . 'Persecutor of Christ . . . Killer of Jesus'?

And my poor father ruining his eyes, forever bent over the insides of cheap watches, giving his last crust of bread away to those bloody relations of mine. Even cousin Reub would not believe the callousness that exists. Or am I being too generous on account of the blood link?

> They are slaves who fear to speak
> For the fallen or the weak,
> They are slaves who do not choose
> Hatred, Suffering or Abuse. . .

Oh, my God, have I had my share of all three? The hatred from the women, the jealous petty female impersonators with their tight calculating little minds and their dependence on men. During the war the way they hounded me from the Overseas Club, poor little me and my poor weak eyes, and still they were jealous of the way the men swarmed after me, me, with a tumour growing inside me the size of a football and still they begrudged me the solace of admiration. Teaching the men English, with my poor little Education (now which University did you attend?), and so witty and gay, giving them all leaflets for the concerts and shows, and crawling, yes crawling back to that concentration camp in Billing Street with Eichmann Hannah waiting for me with his bricks wrapped up in newspaper. And all of them avoiding me in the streets, all, and Reub passing me by without a look, his own blood, and not even a nod of the head, not even the courtesy of an enquiry. Oh, before all that he was glad enough to acknowledge me, when he was a snotty little boy without an overcoat. 'My lovely cousin Shebah,' he would tell all his friends, 'and can we come to the Playhouse club and watch you act? May we, please, dear Shebah?'

What money does to people. What effect it has on their ideals, their loyalties. It couldn't have happened in the old days, it just would not have happened. But now ... now they're all alike.

This lovely house full of marvellous things, rare as peacocks, and Claud throwing his money about on drink and saying he's penniless, and Norman lying there in a suit that must have cost a fortune, though he said he could not afford to travel here in the train, and Maggie supported from first to last by men, however she may deny it, sprawling on the grass with the sole of her shoe worn through, and her skirt held together by a safety pin. We would have been too proud to let the World see our poverty. We would have made something out of nothing and put a bit of lace here and a bit of ribbon there, and still people would have turned their heads to look at us. The hats I made out of bits of curtains and scraps of velvet, and the dresses I made out of oddments, one for every day of the week, and there was not an eye that did not hold regard or envy as I trotted down the street on my dainty little heels. When I tell them they all say in that annoyingly insincere way, 'Oh yes I can believe it', and Victorian Norman turns his head away and I'm supposed not to notice that he's laughing.

But it's true. I was unique. I was beautiful. It's the suffering, the hatred and the abuse that have brought me this low. The aloneness, the rottenness of my relations, the jealousy I have encountered everywhere. If I had received one tenth of their education, their opportunities, what could I not have done with my life, with the brain I have. Maggie's clever, she has a certain quality that I had, that makes people envious, but she uses her mind more cunningly. She wheedles and insinuates, she knows how to make herself indispensable and desirable. I had never her strength though, her sheer animal courage, which does exist, however I may disapprove. To bring up two little children, to take the risks she does, to go here, there and everywhere and have the house full of people, and to manage to appear so soft and gentle and in need of protection. I've told her all this, we even laugh about it. Her in need of protection. There's not a soul that comes within yards of Maggie that does not need protecting from her. That poor man from the College and that young man from America with a head like a cap of fur and such little womanly feet. Now he needed protecting, even if he was Jewish. She likes Jewish men. She likes all men. There she was inviting him to Sunday lunch served on a medley of cracked plates, and—'How do I cook this, Shebah?' and 'How should I make gravy, Shebah?' and all coy when he arrives as if butter wouldn't melt in her mouth. Before that it had been science and atoms and explosions and just like taking off a pair of gloves it's medicine and psychology, and books all over the place on schizophrenia, till we were all demented. Now it's geology and rocks and he, poor Edward, all among the grass smoking his cigarettes (the money they all squander), his blue eyes completely blinded by her, besotted, quite unable to see her true nature. Not that he isn't taking full advantage of the situation. Last night at the table he says it's his birthday, and without a sign of embarrassment he remarks he wants to spend it in bed, and up he gets and off they go. Like a pair of animals.

We went walks along the front at New Brighton, in the wind, in the rain (so beneficial to the complexion) talking, talking about literature, about art, and me in my tight little dress and a piece of fur about my neck, always talking, always walking.

We didn't go to bed all over the place, we hadn't the knowledge, we were so gay, so full of life. What they would talk about now if they hadn't the bed to retire to, God alone knows. Their pathetic bird-droppings of knowledge on books and politics and fashion. Norman with his socialistic outlook, and so concerned about the correct width of his trousers at the calf, and his uncharitable attitude towards me. Oh, I've seen him in the kitchen at Morpeth Street, with his face flushed red, watching the girls, and he and Maggie looking at one another (God knows what goes on there) and then all of a sudden it's 'Good night, All' and he winds up his clock and goes up to bed without a glance. Sometimes he did walk me home I suppose, only Maggie told him to, and latterly I can hardly bring myself to speak to him. The tickets I got him for the Film Institute and the way he said he couldn't afford them, and that anyway he was too busy.

His mother, poor thing, does not understand him at all. Why should her Norman, with a good home, choose to live in one room in Morpeth Street? 'His father and I have never interfered with him at all,' she told me (quite a pretty little woman really, though stupid, though cunning enough to get a man to support her), 'but he always had such strange ideas.' I could have told her, easily enough, what sort of ideas he has, though it wouldn't have done any good, and I have to go somewhere to pass the time.

When I first met Maggie she was such a submissive little thing, all gentle, and soft sighs and looking at her Joseph like a devoted dog. And there she sat playing at being a wife and mother with a fat little baby on her knee like a bowl of shiny fruit, and nursing it and dressing it, and continually giving it her breast to suck on, quite charming I suppose, and then another baby, and dressing and feeding that one, and looking at me when I said 'Where's Joseph?' and saying in that lost child's voice, which is diabolical really . . .

'He doesn't live here any more . . . he's gone.'

Of course I had heard rumours, but the whole place was like a great manure heap of steaming half-truths, and I wasn't sure so I said . . .

'O Maggie, O darling, O no.'

And she says, touching the little fat thing kicking on her lap . . . 'O Shebah, O darling, O yes.'

Just like that. All the time I'd been going there, though I did not see a lot of Joseph, there was never a sign, never a hint or a suggestion. Oh, sometimes she did look a little sad and pale, but then she has got a melancholy cast to her features and plays on it, but I never dreamt that things had gone so far. Though when I told her she disagreed with my choice of words. 'Things,' she said, 'have not gone far. Joseph has merely removed himself further off.' For a moment she looked at me and her eyes held a shadow of such suffering that should it have been real, which I doubt, I might have been forced to change my opinion of her. She can look very ugly and she did then; the face was a triangle of bones, with the naked eyes staring at me under that untidy fringe of hair. Then the baby let loose a little dribble of a cry and she became busy and domestic again. Later on we sang songs though she always gets the words wrong, not like me with my tremendous memory, and she begged me to sing 'The Army of Today's All Right', so I did.

If I had not started to sing last night I might never have touched that glass case, and Claud might not have shot me through the ankle. There is a moment, as I have told them so many times, when everything is too late.

As Maggie told me, in the kitchen, pointing to the absurdly fashionable photograph of herself and the bridesman Joseph—'There was a moment, Shebah, when it became too late. It was to have been all happy endings and Agonisties crowned with flowers' (whatever that might mean—her quotations are always so wildly inaccurate), 'but now I weep alone.' Weep she may have done, but hardly alone. For all that she never took down the photograph from the wall, but left it in its frame alongside all the other pictures and the large painting of the two young girls with white dresses and bows in their hair. Nellie and Doris, Maggie called them, having found the painting in the basement and put it in a gilt frame and a vase of flowers beneath it. All that in a kitchen with the floor riddled with dry rot or wet rot, and a samovar on the draining board, though God knows the only tea she ever made was in a pan and that stewed over and over till in the end I simply could not taste a normal cup of tea. It's all so changed since Maggie went, though Norman has been surprisingly kind. I used to sit in the basket chair under the picture of the cabin boy with his faded midshipman's cap, and opposite the painting of Nellie and Doris. Of course, I do still sit in the chair when I visit Norman, but she took all the pictures away with her. If she wanted to create an impression, though God knows she could hardly fail to do that, Maggie would tell her visitors that she liked to think of Nellie and Doris safely through their dual menopause and dead and buried.

'It gives, don't you think' (a wide candid smile) 'such perspective to our lives?'

And they, the fools, just gaped at her and of course came again and again. Had they known, had they dreamt of the way she would dissect them, once they had left, they would not have thought her quite so innocent, so much the child.

There was another photograph, quite small, of her dead father, hung between a Russian farming family and the entry of the Germans into Vienna. Her poor father, such a polite man and intelligent enough to recognise me as a lady, and there again the general attitude was so bewildering, so eccentric.

I thought of Maggie all that long fog-wreathed day, as I struggled through the streets hardly able to breathe, nearly knocked down by a number twelve bus, mourning with her, saying a little prayer for the departed. And to arrive later that night at Morpeth Street and the kitchen crowded and Maggie with a fur hat on and a blanket and a pair of Wellington boots, and behaving as if she were drunk, which she may have been. Not one expression of sorrow, not one tear, not one glance of respect or sympathy, only an air of hilarity, of Thanksgiving. And Mrs Ryan and I shedding a little pity over the table for fathers lost and fathers gone (though hers by the sound of him was no great loss to the bogs of Ireland) and I remembered, if indeed I had ever forgotten, how I was ill for so many weeks when my dear father died. There was so much laughing and Lizzie had been attacked coming through the streets and Norman had given her a sip of brandy (the money they throw about) and Maggie told a dreadful story about how her father had sometimes not spoken for months and how the Vicar said he was such a jolly man. Sitting there in that fur hat of hers, with lines of dirt about her mouth, drinking stewed tea and loving it all. Because of the fog no one could go home and they all paired off like animals as usual, and I was told to go and lie down on the sofa (Mrs Ryan for some reason having been pressed to take the brass bed), and when I left Maggie was lying on a lilo on the kitchen floor in her hat and boots singing, 'Oh, it's nice to have a Home of your Own'. I don't mean to be critical, she can be a kind child, but sometimes her callousness is appalling. I won't say she has been callous to me, not really, though I daresay she can be behind my back, and having heard her views on all her friends, so called, I don't see why I should be exempt, but she does tend to adopt a different attitude in front of different people. Claud for instance seemed to bring out the worst in her. He used to arrive without warning at Morpeth Street. Just to get into his yellow motor car and drive all those miles and arrive with bottles of this and bottles of that, and for days Maggie would be laughing and shouting, altogether too elated. Of course elation is only the extreme end of deep depression, but how she kept going all through the day with the children to care for, and the telephone ringing, and rifling the gas meters for money to buy eggs and tea, and the nights spent in abandonment, and that dreadful Miss Charters taking tea every afternoon. I came one afternoon because I was passing the door and wanted to make sure of my appointment with Maggie for the evening, and there was Claud in the kitchen stretched out on my chair with a glass in front of him and 'Hallo, my dear, you look well'—me, hardly able to lift my head for the pain and the tragedy of everything, the ignorant swine—and this old, old creature with bedroom slippers on its feet, and hands caked with dirt, rocking back and forth like a rag doll, showing what the children call her dangerous teeth, and Maggie saying so sweet and nice and pie and so insincerely: 'Shebah, this is a friend of mine, Miss Charters' ... as if in some way we had something in common. Oh, I felt pity for the poor old thing, so neglected and so idiotic, asking me if my daddy went to sea, but they simply don't see the difference between my suffering with the brain I've got, and these other vermin who barely inhabit the earth. I wish to God I could wallow in my muck and accept all that England has to offer. I did try but I could not bring myself to talk to her at all, and afterwards Maggie said I had been impolite to Miss Charters, and Claud gave a little high-pitched laugh and began to whistle between his teeth. I cannot afford to be too rude to Maggie but sometimes I would like to tell her dear devoted friends exactly what she thinks of them behind their backs. Oh, I know it was kind of Claud to invite me here, even if it was only for target practice, but I have done my share of entertaining, I have ceaselessly provided them with knowledge. And there was the train fare and peppermints for Julia and chocolate drops for the children, and I did sit and pat those damn dogs for half an hour.

It could have been so charming, this weekend, in this ideal setting, all so beautifully furnished and the pictures everywhere and the cut glass, but almost from the moment we arrived there were undertones and atmospheres and one or other of them would vanish into another room and whisper away, or there would be looks at each other, and those tedious half-finished sentences, like the half of a letter you find in the street, that you can't make head nor tail of, no matter how you try. It's as if all this fascination with sex builds a big wall betwixt the devotees and the non-devotees. If you are not a participant there is simply so much that is incomprehensible. They pretend to be interested in Art and politics and books, and they seem to chat quite intelligently for a time, but always, like a maggot eating its way across a particularly decayed and juicy fruit, there's this sexual business, leaving a small trail of slime, and nothing else seems to really bring them to life. I do see, now that Maggie has explained it to me, that it's not entirely what it seems. Even I can see their motives are somewhat different, but their impulses all seem to be working in unison, and they all pretend so much to emotions that must surely be real only once, that must be true only the first time, not over and over like a ball unable to stop bouncing.

When we came through the door of the shop yesterday, Claud put his arms round Maggie and they clung there among all those breakable things set out on mahogany tables, mouths emitting sucking noises, and Julia behind them, so courteous, so well bred. To look at her you would never dream she was a mistress, that she too was indulging so vividly and with such ladylike capability in this orgy of shared eroticism, night after night taking off her spectacles and brushing her hair, and rub rub rubbing at those lovely teeth, each one sitting in the pink gums fair and square and milky, and after that God knows what madness. The way they all attend to their teeth, as if they were the gates to some sort of parkland. Reub has good teeth, though he speaks with his lips close together, spitting out his facts and figures and percentages, and once when he had the generosity to take me over the road for a cup of coffee, he yawned, and the fascinating glimpse of the mauve lining of his mouth and the back molars pitted with gold.

I ought to have my teeth attended to, I really ought, but, oh, the shame of exposing the private altogether too intimate cavities of the jaw to some jumped-up little dentist boy, and I can't quite see myself going round with a mouth full of dentures, artificial, snapping like a mad dog, and they would have to be kept decent and cleaned day and night and it's all too much trouble for poor me. It's all too loose in there. It's like a purse with the lining in threads. I have seen Maggie spewing blood out after she's cleaned her teeth at night, and mixing stuff in a glass and swilling it round her mouth and tears starting from her eyes.

She does look ill. It's all this racketing about and not eating properly and rushing from place to place. It's extraordinary how particular they are about their emotions and their teeth and yet they simply never eat a decent meal or sleep regularly. Oh, Julia did provide a very nice meal for us last night, though it was ruined by the conversation. When I think of how my poor mother prepared a meal, such care, such bravery in the face of adversity. Not that she would stoop to cook anything so simple as shepherd's pie. And the wine Claud kept offering them all running like water, and the indiscreet sentences tossed betwen them. . . .

'It's a bloody wonderful life,' said Norman. He's right there, it is for him with his weekly wage and his doting mother.

'You mean that?' Claud the fool stares entranced as if discovering great wisdom.

'Yes. Yes, I do. I live, I make love to as many women as possible, I eat well, I climb mountains. I've good friends and we had a damn good time altogether in Morpeth Street.'

'I reckon,' said Claud, for some reason agreeing with Norman, 'that you're right. I reckon love-making is about all a man should want. That and drink, eh?'

With a boozy surge of laughter they raised their glasses up to be refilled and listened to his oratory.

'I reckon that in order for the blood to flow, we must have real stimulation. It's all right for some people, with their diamond minds. . . .'

'Oh, darling,' I cried, for who else could he have meant but me, staring at me like that with his sweet crazy eyes . . . 'but the rest of us ordinary mortals need something in which to sublimate ourselves. Some way in which we can release our inhibitions and return to the soil.'

The words evidently had an effect on Maggie's young man. He stood up so calmly, as if asking to leave the table, and commanded Maggie to go to bed with him. There and then, without any more ado. Wanted to celebrate his birthday, he said, in the most fitting way. And Maggie sitting there with a little satisfied smile as if he were paying her a compliment instead of insulting her. And we were left sitting round the table in the kitchen, talking trivialities and they drinking their wine, and me feeling so weary and far too polite to mention it.

'Come, come, Shebah,' Claud said, 'the night is young,' and I could not disagree with him, being a guest in his house, even if I was shot down like a bird of prey, and it would only imply that I was not young.

And I am young, younger by far than them. I used to sit up all night during the war, in the shelters, and when even that poor refuge was denied me by the attitude of the scum who came there, I would huddle in a blanket on my little divan high above the street, a sort of Jewish barrage balloon, my stomach all swollen with the tumour inside me. I did have my own little room (though I did only move there just for somewhere to put my things, never intending to stop twenty years), with all my books on the shelves, some with inscriptions written just inside the cover in his handwriting. 'Did you ever have a love affair?' asked Claud last night. Did I ever have a love affair? You'd think they had a monopoly on love. Maybe not what they would call an affair, though that did happen once, but it was a romantic affair, and it was more than enough for me. How they stand the repeated strain on the nerves and the intrigue and the heartache I cannot imagine, let alone the echo they must evoke deep within their minds of similar words uttered in similar situations and for similar ends. My affair was so rich in texture, so varied in its detail.

There I sat at a play-reading and the hall was in darkness because that was the way Jerry wanted it done and I was reciting some lines and he heard my voice, and he said to a friend, there and then in the pitch blackness: 'My God, who is she? I must know her.' He had seen me about of course, everybody had, and I was so different and so chic, but we had not actually spoken and after that night he bought me flowers and we sat for hours talking about poetry, and such a sombrous face, a dark face with studious eyes, and so tall and educated. When I think of those things Maggie called men, who used to court her, that little toad of an American, Joel or Moley or something, and that professor all fourteen stone of chasmy fat, or that Billie with his schoolboy face and beblubbered eyes, in comparison with him, I smile. She doesn't know what a man is. And I wouldn't let him buy me as much as a cup of tea, because I was too proud, and the night he introduced me to his wife I was so charming and she said to him later ... 'I love Shebah, you should love Shebah too. She is so different, so alive.' Of course, all the other hags in the readers' circle were jealous of me and would not speak to me, a positive gathering up of the folds of the skirts if I came too near, and all the men flocked round me and thought me something I most definitely was not. I wonder what stopped me. I could have been like Maggie. God knows I flirted enough, I was so gay, so painfully exhilarated. And those great eyes of mine, thoral eyes, he said, though I never gave that a thought, giving me such hell even then, but I was too vain to wear glasses, though I was almost blind. The pain I endured. He thought I was weeping and observed I was too tender for this world, which in a way I was, am, though it was just my eyes were so damn weak.

The day I came into the club, long after we had severed our association, and the men were sitting by the fire talking and one said, because he knew, they all knew: 'Isn't it terrible, Shebah?' and I said:

'What?' and he said:

'Why, he's gassed himself, Shebah.'

And then I did weep and I don't care what they thought. I never liked Jewish men. Never. Always the Christian boys. Besides my poor father would never have been able to give me a dowry and I hated the idea of being bought. And the Christian men were too stupid mostly, except him, though there was probably a touch of the Jew there, with those eyes, and I could never understand women wanting to have children. The responsibility. The strength they all have. And then there's always the worry. That time Maggie nearly died, though she never told me the full story, how she coped with the worry I'll never know. And no sooner is she through with all that than she meets the American with his stony face and I warned her and said, because I do have a deep regard for her even if I think her a damn fool, 'Don't give yourself to him, darling.'

And she laughed with those innocent eyes shining like baubles and says ... 'Why, Shebah, I love him, I love him.' At least that what she called it. There she is asking me round to Sunday dinner and 'how do you make gravy, Shebah?' and 'have you brought the black bread?' and setting out the food on three cracked plates and music on the gramophone and not a mention of Billie and all that love.

Oh no, it's all schizophrenia and the mid-brain and diseases of the kidney from morning till night, and arguments about the medical service both here and on the Continent, and such coy-ness. Though what he made of it all I don't know. Thought he was in a typically British household, God help him, and quite bewildered and glassy-eyed with Victorian Norman spouting Communism at him, and that dreadful man Rafferty arriving drunk and begging to see Our Kid and telling everyone he's a navy man, and Claud coming in his frock coat to commit suicide and the professor breaking his atomic heart on the front step. And he had the cheek to tell me I was completely SANE. Poor little me with my tragic life and all the torment visiting the out-patients' department every week. 'Have you ever,' he asked me, 'had a day by the sea?' A day by the sea. The poor little fool. Of course, Maggie made out he was a doctor but what the hell did he know? Anyway all the professor's darling books on neutrons we parcelled up and then we had volumes all over the place on Elation and new approaches to Manic Depressives, and God knows I've been one of those for years without having books on it, and case books on Psycho-Analysis until no one hardly ever spoke, just came in and sat down and started reading and imagining all sorts of things. Everyone had such terrible childhoods and no one had experiences any more, only traumas. Not that he made us very welcome all the time he was around. Just standing, all four feet of him by the sink, with folded arms, the breathing example of an inferiority complex, saying Yeah and Nope to whatever one said, and no sense of humour at all. Then when he had gone and the light had gone out of her eyes, she seemed worried again and it might have been that, though of course she's so deep and she never told me.

There's something wrong now but I don't suppose I'll be permitted to know. If only she knew how trustworthy I am! I did think last night Claud was going to confide in me but he didn't tell me very much. 'Come Shebah,' he says, and I prepared myself for one of his ridiculous conversations which are not conversations at all but recitations of his wife leaving him (and God knows one can hardly blame her) and the great glory that is Maggie, and a few flatteries thrown at me, just as if I cannot see through him, or any of them. And there was Victorian Norman with his arm around Julia whilst she washed the dishes.

'Shall I help you, darling?' I said, bloody fool that I am, hardly able to stand, and offering to clean their china for them.

'No, thank you, Shebah,' she says, dry mouth impeccably shaping her vowels, steam from the bowl blurring her glasses so that I could not see her expression, though I can imagine. Wanted me out of the way so as to be alone with Norman.

When I used to help at the Overseas Club during the war the rotten women were so jealous of me. All the young men wanted to talk with me, to be with Shebah. 'Teach us to speak English, Shebah,' they would say, 'you speak English so beautifully.'

And those women with their wretched little brains saying ... 'No, thank you, Shebah, there's nothing for you to do, we can manage.' They're all alike, God forgive them.

So Claud and I go upstairs, under that angel made of wood, into the long living room and he puts on the gramophone (how they all dote on noise) and I settle myself on the sofa. There was a little time taken up with those moist dogs and I had to pat them and he kept saying 'Lie down', all the time inciting them to jump around with saliva dripping in such abundance from their great purple jaws, and I went on laughing and making soothing noises, though really I wanted to scream. After a time he got tired of all that and they put their noses into the carpet and went off to sleep.... 'Dear Shebah,' he said, 'how you observe us all ... how wise you are.' He really is a most interesting man even if he did shoot me down in the grass. A puckish face, rather creased, and merry eyes and that beard in little curls so that he constantly licks out at tendrils with his tongue, and a small mouth, very pink. How young they all look in spite of their complications. So deeply healthy.

'What me?' I said, because I detest insincere flattery, and he wagged his head, which is a whimsical habit and repeated ...

'How wise you are' ... and stares down at my feet. At the end of my legs (oh, my shapely legs that danced so much, that walked so far) I could see my sandals swing above the carpet and my little toes peeping out, and a dab of sealing wax that was really red nail varnish blobbing one toe and just visible through my stocking. My pathetic adornments. Reub said it was the harlot in me, the swine.

'What about you,' I trilled, 'with all this beauty around you, and your wonderful knowledge—aren't you wise?'

Which certainly was not wise of me because it meant he

could start on his wife leaving him etc., etc., but I had to say something, After a while he said: 'You see the wise ones are those who no longer fight against life, but accept and observe.' And he licked at his beard again and pushed at one of the dogs with his foot, though mercifully it remained unconscious. I keep trying to tell Maggie this, it's just something they cannot understand. They all do say some very clever things and very important things, but their method of delivery is so bad. Being an actress I say things with conviction. They never sound as if they believe what they say. You do have to dramatise when making the profounder statements. And he looks so well fed and so cushioned with grandeur that it's simply absurd to think of him fighting against anything. What on earth is there for him to object to? If only he had paused or sighed in the appropriate place I would have been more convinced. I know he has had his troubles, his sufferings, though God knows he's done it in comfort, in opulence, but the art of conversation is communication and communication is a thing that must be felt. The spoken word seems to have lost its meaning. With all this television any little chit of a nothing walking the streets can mouth about life and suffering. That girl in the Kardomah some months ago, with her hair bleached and frizzed about her ears, quite attractive really, and her smooth little face without expression.

I had gone in for a cup of tea (I have to sit somewhere and the G.P.O. was about to close and I was too early for my next appointment and so weary) and there was this common man sitting by the wall, slouched in his chair, with a face stamped with brutality and weakness like they all bear marks of now, being kept and housed and fed by England and no need to work at all. I had not been there for more than a few moments and I brought the edge of my cup to my mouth, and was about to drink, when I saw him put two spoons and a knife into the pocket of his jacket. He saw me looking at him and we stared at one another, a quite exquisite second of perception, me with my cup held up and he with his hand curled round the cutlery in his pocket, and all the little café sounds about us, hot water rushing out of the urn, and saucers being rattled and an isolation of recognition between this sot and myself. Then he got up, still with his eyes fixed on mine and in a moment I was standing by the exit with my poor weak arms outstretched, weary as I was. Nobody moved, though people looked up from their crumbling buns. 'No you don't,' I shouted. 'Thief, taker of property.' The fools on the counter just stared at me, lifeless, immobile. 'He's put Kardomah cutlery into his pocket, two spoons and a knife, I saw him. Call the manager.' I knew there wasn't much point in calling the manager because he was most likely upstairs threshing about among the cardboard boxes and sacks of sugar, commingling with one of the women assistants, and the man, the thief, just moved forward and took hold of my arm and thrust me roughly aside, and in a moment he was in the revolving doors and round and out with a damp rush of air into the darkling street. Just went, and nobody came to my assistance; down went the insensitive heads to the currant scones and the mugs of tea, and this little fool with the dyed and curled hair, as transparent as a piece of glass, said softly in a voice distorted with catarrh . . .

'Oh, give him a chance. Aren't you human?'

Just that. Aren't you human? Had it been reversed, had it been I who had stolen so much as a crust of bread, they would have trampled on me, risen in a pyramid of loathing from the tables and ground me to the floor, called me a dirty Jew, cast me into prison. It was on account of the feeling and the emotion that I put into my accusation that they hated me. They sat still with an embarrassment that turned them to stone. It is the generation of the unemphatic. Steal, kill, lie, fornicate, but beware of indulging with conviction. That's their idea of being human.

Anyway, Claud is quite wrong. I've never stopped fighting. I've never accepted so much as a cup of water. I've fought all my life for justice and been broken and destroyed in its cause. However, I suppose Claud was meaning to pay me a compliment and I couldn't tell him to go to bloody hell as I would have liked to have done, being a guest in his house of china, so I contented myself with: 'O darling . . . me . . . accepting . . . how little you know.' Which of course only made him feel how humble I was, though as usual with all of them I got the impression he was only half concentrating, that he was waiting or listening for something else. If I wasn't so subtle I would long ago have decided they were all deliberately trying to humiliate and torment me, which is true in a way, but really it's their thoughtlessness and their preoccupation with sex.

To which he replied, fiddling and tugging at his curled beard

... 'Very true, my dear, very true. How little I know. But this I do know. Whilst we have sat on this sofa this five minutes, twelve people somewhere have died of hunger. Died starving.'

I want to scream when they start talking this way. It's so debasing. Are they talking to me or to themselves? Do I look as if I'm one of the privileged, that they have to relate the statistics of little yellow people or brown people clutching rice bowls? It's not my concern. I have enough to battle with in my own monstrous head without problems of that sort. Not that they do anything about the hungry either. It's all talk. And if I haven't starved to death it's no thanks to anybody but myself. I haven't been lend-leased or subsidised, and I don't have the solace of their endless involvements. I've had nothing but lone-liness and jealousy and ill health. I feel as if I'm constantly struggling under a net cast carelessly by a careless God. I'm the only one I know enmeshed in it, all the others move freely. The appalling thing is that nobody seems aware of my plight.

Once, when that landlord of mine, the Panzer man in the tennis pumps, had thrown bricks at me, I ran out screaming into the road. 'Help, murder,' I shouted. People passed by on foot with shut faces, and people went past in the glass cabins of their cars, eyes luminous and unseeing, and no one lifted a finger of surprise, no black pupil enlarged at the image of my suffering. The landlord came down the steps with his bicycle under his arm and propped it against the railings whilst he fixed his cycle clips round the frayed bottoms of his trousers. He then mounted his machine, and the white tennis shoes, black laces dangling, trod round and round on the pedals and carried him out of sight. He of course had his own sedatives, his rotten Irish Catholic candle-lighting, and his paid women that came nightly, spiking up the uncarpeted stairs in their high-heeled shoes, their very breathing sulphurous with cor-ruption. But I have nothing, no compensations, no curtain of deceit to hide myself from myself. Only my poor brain endlessly facing itself. Claud's remark was only to be expected, because they always make such comments, so I should not have felt so irritated, so exhausted with bitterness. Knowing so much, my bitterness can only be self-directed, their being nobody worthier to receive it. I had to sit there nodding agreement, rolling my eyes whilst the blood pounded in my head. There was a small silence in which the record ended. Maggie had a gramophone in the kitchen, and two records which she played every evening. The battery on my nerves was simply frightful. It's not that I cannot enjoy music, who better, but my appointments were for communication, as I used to tell her, not to have to shout my thoughts above a cyclone on violins. I didn't want Claud to put on another orchestral work, so I said as quickly as I could before he noticed the silence—'Do you think, Claud darling, that Edward is right for her?'

Then he said a most extraordinary thing. I suppose it was only extraordinary in that there is so much I am never told. It's like trying to complete a jig-saw. They toss me all the edges but never the most vital pieces in the centre.

'It's not a question of rightness, Shebah. He's needed very much. And I reckon in some ways he'll do.'

'What do you mean—needed?' I hate begging them for explanations, but I was so taken by surprise.

'Well ...' He pursed up his little wet mouth and let his chin rest on his chest so that his face was mostly beard and there were plumes of auburn hair springing out of his scalp. Then up comes his head and he puts a large hand on my black-skirted knee and stares at me intently. Really quite dramatic considering what they are usually like. 'Don't we all need someone, or something?' he says, the fool, the sly antique dealer, talking to me as if I worked in a factory or was one of those ignorant little things he picks up in his yellow van. They do belittle my intelligence so. He meant of course something different, but until Maggie actually confides in me, or until the faint rumours begin to circulate, I'll never know. Which left me in pain again. Suffocating pain, because I have no outlet for my passion, and the less I can project my passion into words, the more I sense the threat of nothingness. And then he began to talk about the glory that is Maggie, which was interesting in one way and not entirely drivel. He said: 'Of us all, Maggie needs nobody. I say this guardedly. The rest of us can find our little treadwheel and go round and round because basically all we care about is stupefying ourselves. Intensity of life can be found equally well in business or in drink.'

Here I said sharply, because I wasn't going to let him get away with it ... 'And the so-called loving you all indulge in?'

Here his eyes flickered, once, twice, beneath lids tinted pink. He removed his large hand from my knee and commenced to tug at his beard worriedly. 'No, no, Shebah, that's something quite different. We none of us indulge, as you call it, for the reasons you believe. Some for loneliness, some for forgetfulness, some because they are endlessly chosen.' The skin of his face was not after all so very young, so extremely healthy. No blood flowed under the surface, only the mouth glistened as the pale flat tongue lubricated the lower lip. 'But, you see, Maggie has chosen life. She is the self-creator of her own struggling, her own griefs, her own happiness. She endures self-loss only to fling herself triumphantly back into an emotional battle to regain herself. She will not, she cannot, seeing she is the only contestant, give in. That is the glory of her.'

Well, I couldn't laugh out loud in his hair circumferenced face and I had not the energy to start a futile discussion, so I again nodded my poor aching head, and he seemed satisfied and with a little sigh, whether real or assumed, stood up and went downstairs trailing his hand on the surface of the wall.

The rubbish they talk. Maggie has chosen life. She is the self-creator. It's almost as if he thought Maggie religious. Of course she is a Catholic, or was, though that was probably a decision taken on impulse. All that business of riding on a tram up or down a hill to a convent in the mist, and joining the Nuns at prayer, and letting salt tears run down her cheeks. How her senses must have grovelled before the little lighted candles and the rising voices, really not unlike Blackpool during the illuminations, and the incense burning and imagining herself full of transport and divine grace. Her whole existence is a catalogue of sensual indulgences. She has never self-created anything, only gone blindly into any situation that presented itself. I was there that night the Billie man called on some pretext. I was sitting in the kitchen by appointment and long before the knock came she confided that somebody might arrive, no one of any importance she stressed, purely a matter of business, but would I mind going upstairs and resting on the bed in the bathroom for a little time, should a visitor come. And before she would open the door I was bundled upstairs with all my parcels and my carrier bag, still holding a plate of stew in my hand and hardly able to see in the badly-lit hall. I could hear voices and then there was some banging and then there was silence. I stayed up there as long as I could, as long as was humanly possible, what with the cold and all the insane people rushing in to use the lavatory and their insane comments, and when I did go back into the kitchen, the panel under the sink was open and there was water all over the floor and on the floor amidst the potato peelings and the swillage, Maggie and her Billie. Such a different Maggie from the one half an hour before, great eyes shining, mouth curved in a tender smile, really very pretty, with her skirt marked and stained with tea leaves, and he the great fool, red in the face and a piece of sticking plaster on his dimpled chin, and such a seductive insincere voice. I never liked him. When he had gone she sat with her face in her hands, amidst all that mess, rocking backwards and forwards. 'I love him,' she said, though she wasn't telling me, 'I love him.' Jumping on a chair and moaning through her teeth—'O I love him, I love him.' Since that time she's jumped on the same chair quite a few times and repeated the same sentiments, only about different people. The fact that she emerges triumphantly, as Claud describes it, out of all these situations, is not courage but luck. Supreme good fortune. And the opportunities she has had. I sat there last night quite alone, and only a few yards away lay Maggie with her latest lover, adrift in each other's arms. God knows what passes through her mind at such moments. There was never anywhere I could go. I couldn't get up from the table and announce I was spending a birthday in bed; I possessed no friends who openly encouraged me.

I went all the way to London so many years ago, by coach, with Monica Sidlow (she hated me too, with her over-active glands that deposited fat all over her hips and thighs) and we stayed at some theatrical boarding house for one night, before she went on to Paris. What a sight she looked pouring water into a basin, great arms a-flurry with flesh, and the short muscular legs bare and pallid under the laced camisole. I could have gone to Paris with her, only even then there did not seem any difference—Paris, London, all one—I had to take myself with me wherever I went. My love, my married man, with the grey calm eyes and the wife who had after all told him to adore me, was coming down by car alone to fetch me, and when he did come I stood as if facing an army, a whole regiment of enemies with loaded guns pointing at my breast, with a fearful excitement building up inside me, and I shouted—'Don't dare touch me'—so violently that people in the street turned to look at us.

And he, one lone grenadier, his noble face white in the hurrying street, said-pleaded-entreated: 'What do you want, Shebah? For God's sake what do you want?'

He had a coat (he always dressed most beautifully) made of some dark textured cloth, and the fingers of his right hand touched nervously the lapels, whilst he stood looking at me. I said, still shouting: 'Nothing, nothing from you,' and he turned away and walked very slowly to his big green car, and I did not wait to see him drive away, but buttoned up my little black gloves and pushed the fur of my collar higher around my ears and trotted as fast as my legs would carry me into the unknown crowds. My exultation was for a time so magnificent that I could have walked all day, but gradually the feeling left me and my mouth became dry, and I was after all alone, having accomplished a gesture of nothingness. Why, I ask myself, after all this time? Of course, I did want something from him, I suppose I was in love with him. Of course, he wasn't mine, he did belong to his wife, and in those days that counted for much, but it wasn't entirely that. Perhaps it's because I am bigger than anyone I have ever met. There is so much of me that there is no room for transference. Perhaps it's the Jewish wandering element in me. A wanderer over the face of the earth. As a baby, a tiny Hebrew-nosed infant, with weak eyes closed shut, my mother carried me across Russia. And what hell she went through with my father's relations. Always walking, always on the move. Even now I cannot keep still, I have to keep going, even if it's only round and round the blackened streets of the town. I could never tell Maggie (because though she might be moved by its symbolic beauty at the time of telling, later she would repeat it to all and sundry, and distort its meaning beyond recall) but it is his coat I remember now more than his face, which I don't remember. His lovely dark majestic coat. I am truly the self-creator of my own struggles. Impulsive it may appear, but underneath there is an inflexible will that guides my destiny. That's my great glory, damn, damn them.

I wondered last night what was up between Norman and Julia. She seems very sweet, but you never know and Norman is capable of anything. Maggie has told me that Norman is the only man she has ever met who wanted sex for the real reason, what she calls the biological urge. If she told Claud that it's a wonder he left Julia alone with him, though perhaps he wouldn't mind. They're all so deep. Why now, should he shoot me this morning? I don't get the impression, though I could be wrong, that Claud has an inflexible will that rules his existence. And if he has it would not seem enough reason to aim a gun at poor me with my countless torments, and pull the trigger. I have not done him so much harm, and if I have it was his fault forcing me to drink, though if I had not drunk I would have wept.

After our little discussion last night he was downstairs quite a little while. It was quite pleasant sitting there among all those marvellous bits and pieces. I was slightly anxious in case the dogs woke up and started their antics, but I sat very still with my hands folded, and when Claud came back up the stairs with Norman and Julia (both very elated and gay) he shouted out ... 'Ho, my dear, you look like an African carving ... better have a drink.' Norman was laughing a great deal and wriggling about in his clothes and blowing his nose over and over into a spotless handkerchief. The noise he made.

'We're going to sing "Happy Birthday" to the loved ones,' shouted Claud, filling up glasses on the piano top.

So we all trooped to the door and down two little steps and stood outside another door, very old, with a great iron hinge (everything's too perfect) and Claud started up the chorus. We made a great volume of sound, but I'm not so unobservant not to notice how close Victorian Norman was standing to Julia, and how his fingers kept digging into her neck, and all the time shouting at the top of his voice ... 'Happy Birthday, dear Edward' ... a regular synaxis by friends, so-called, and very stimulating, and even I felt slightly absorbed, because it was an absorbing thing to do, disturbing them like that.

Behind the door I could hear Maggie laughing. Of course, she had to laugh just to show there was no ill-feeling and Claud put his hand on the latch of the door and would have gone in, only Julia said protestingly ... 'No, Claud, no' ... and we all went back into the other room still singing. It was so simple to have another drink; it was all so exciting. And I felt that way I might be more included, not so dreadfully impaled about by my own character and personality.

'Why don't you sing Maggie's song?' said Norman, damn him, hunching his narrow shoulders and walking rapidly up and down the room. So I did. Heaven knows I have sung it often enough in the past. I sang it because I like it to have a rousing chorus, though I think to Maggie it represented a kind of comfort to the heart. Years ago Maggie invited me round for the evening of our Day of Atonement. It wasn't my usual appointment night but she said come round anyway, because she can be kind, and all my people have deserted me, and it was a time of great sadness for me, and when I went into the kitchen there were candles and hanging from the ceiling a gaudy red star made out of shiny paper, a Christmas decoration, and I felt like saying 'I'm a Jew, not a Communist', and on the table plates with little rolls on them with scraps of sardines inside, and a gherkin on a saucer, and on the draining board a bottle of whisky and a bottle of wine. So typical to have spent so much on drink and so little on food.

'Oh, darling,' I said, 'why the celebration?' All my people were fasting and praying that night but she just smiled and said:

'Happy birthday, Shebah' (what fools they all are), and I put my bundles down on the green velvet chair, absolutely mesmerised by that great shining scarlet star, hanging on a thread of cotton from a hook in the stained ceiling. 'I have a surprise for you,' she told me, and led me up the hall and into the living room and there on the purple sofa, lying reading a book, was Claud with a thin emaciated face, appearing almost holy. Of course, I knew he had been sick, but I had thought he was in some sort of mental home, and he said, quite unlike himself:

'Hallo, Shebah,' and gravely looked at me out of saintly eyes. He looked as if he was some figure on a tomb, with his two little feet neatly together and his beard in a little point, and a gown in neat folds about his body. It was all so unexpected and people kept arriving and bringing things, chocolate raisins and bottles of wine and a bag of nuts, and them all wishing me Happy Birthday in that insane way and getting very drunk.

We had to stay in the kitchen on account of Claud needing peace and quiet, but one or other of us would trip along every now and then the dark hall length to the cool of his lying-in room, and we all thought how changed he was, how like St Sebastien, St Joseph or Christ, all except Maggie who refused to comment, just went on drinking wine and talking to her American by the sink, with his arms folded, hardly uttering a word. Poor devil, arrested against the draining board, subjugated to Maggie and ten thousand dreams of American superiority tinkling invisibly to ruin among the debris in the sink. He wouldn't go and see Claud at all. Once when Maggie was about to take some bread to him, he said in that inhuman drawl ... 'I reckon he's had enough attention' ... and she ate the roll herself. Of course, she always does adopt this complacent feminine attitude with all her lovers which may fool them but hardly fools me. Victorian Norman was on the floor, almost under the table with Lizzie's friend Patricia, quite a refined girl in many ways, whispering into her ear with the perspiration running down his face. Lizzie was sitting on her boy-friend's knee, really a very sweet girl, though just like all of them. And Maggie so fond of her, which is strange because she is quite pretty, and in the end I expect she'll do Maggie down. They all do. I never liked Lizzie's boy-friend, not a nice man, almost dreadful but saved by a sense of humour, always more than ready to insult me. He sang 'The Holly and the Ivy' in a trained voice, shifting his eyes from side to side throughout, a cup of whisky clasped in his hand. Then I sang 'Let's Start All Over Again', and they clapped and made loud noises of appreciation, all except the American Statue of Liberty, who gazed coldly at us out of sloe-shaped eyes, dry as prunes. Of course, he was Jewish. Little Lizzie went in to see Claud and was away rather a long time and the boy-friend padded along the hall to fetch her; voices were raised in anger, then they both returned, he with a face suffused with annoyance, saying Claud wasn't all that sick, and she patting his crimson cheeks mouthing 'There, there', as if comforting a child. They all have so much physical contact. The whole evening hours went by in a rustle of undeciphered murmurings, a tracery of fingers endlessly stroking heads of hair, and lengths of arm; a dozen licentious violet mouths pursed up to imprint kisses on each other. Winding together, all of them, even poor saintly Claud new to his mortification, touching, clinging, reaching. How apart I sat, how alien. They all lived coupled lives and I alone am singular, isolated. Of course, the professor when he was visiting Maggie didn't maul her in front of me, but then he was too bewildered. He used to come sometimes for lunch and coincide with the policeman. No one ever explained why the policeman called. Surely not him as well. Feeding Boy with a spoon, with his helmet on the draining board, a real man in blue, with silver buttons immaculate, making himself quite at home. He used to chain his cycle to the railings outside and Norman said we should be thankful he wasn't in the mounted division. The professor sat locked in a prison of detachment, an obstruction in his throat not allowing him to speak, the vast body overlapping the upright chair, only the eyes alert, dismayed, drowned in their own philandering, accepting the mug of stewed tea with disbelief, whilst Maggie supreme in her slum kitchen hummed for my benefit something from Gilbert and Sullivan, a smile of exquisite correctness on her assassin's face. She always has a line of song for every occasion, sung badly of course but comical. She told me the day she was born, the moment of entry, the Bolton Borough Band were on the wireless and a Mr Gearn was giving a euphonium solo. All lies but very interesting, And she said miles away in the Llay Main Colliery in Wales under the earth a boy was working and just as her mother shuddered in the final birth pangs, a piece of steel flew out of a wedge and opened his jugular vein, so that he expired on the instant. I suppose it is possible. She asked me when I was born. She was bored because for once there were no men calling and though she does pretend to be cultural she has no consistency, and we sat over that blue oilcloth on the table and wrote things down on a scrap of paper. She's so convincing that I did begin to tremble slightly with a kind of excitement, as if there would really be some clue as to why my life has been one of such suffering and torment. I was a bit wary at first of giving the true year of my birth. It sounded so ancient, so pre-existence, October 29th, 1899. I flounced a little into my handbag and kept asking her questions but she finally made me tell her and I regretted it immediately, because I'm sure she's told everybody. I don't know why she makes me tell her things. God knows, no one else would even dare to ask. Anyway, she wrote down the date and then counted on her fingers (there seem such gaps in her education) and looked up knowingly ... 'Ah, that's interesting. Three nines are most interesting' ... What rubbish. 'Why, darling?' I said, humouring her, but all the same there was a little bead of terror and delight rolling minutely through my bloodstream. 'Well, it leaves 18 and 2 which makes 20.' At least she added it up correctly. 'So take 20 from the three nines or 27 and what have we got?' 'We've got seven left,' I said, whilst the pencil went on doodling across the paper. She was drawing a great clump of flowers in and out of all the dates.

'Exactly. So at seven years of age there was a great change in your life, and one that influenced you for years that followed.' Of course, I must have told her at some time how my poor father left London and came to the North just before my seventh birthday, and how I went to the Hebrew school and how I felt I was forever doomed to unhappiness. That it was the year I knew I was unique and singled out for some great destiny. Of course, I never imagined just what kind of destiny. I thought it was something glorious, something miraculous. I did not dream greatness was a word that could be equally well applied to states of poverty and misery. However, I said ... 'Go on, darling, that is clever' ... though clever it was not.

'What hour were you born?' she asked, staring at me as if she believed I was mesmerised by her. I can never tell if she is acting or not. 'In the afternoon,' I said, though God knows if I was correct. Who the bloody hell cares now, certainly not my poor dear mother gone beyond recall. There I was, an orphan, for all I had been born of parents in 1899, talking such rubbish with a chit of a girl whose egotism is only exceeded by mine.

'Well,' she went on, 'let me see.' And there was a little silence during which I may have laughed scornfully though now I cannot remember. 'Right,' she said quite loudly, and sat up straight and laid her pencil down on the piece of paper. 'At the moment of near birth two cousins chose to marry not far from your home. An Albert Cohen and a Georgina Goldberg. They stood in the Empress Rooms at the Kensington Palace Hotel and were married by the Rabbi and two assistants. At the Lyceum Henry Irving was applying powder to his brow during the matinée interval of *Robespierre*. At the Shaftesbury Theatre the stage was being swept for the evening performance of the *Belle of New York*. The Boers had been bombarding Mafeking for two hours, and would continue to do so for another two, managing to kill one dog, breed unknown. The dear Queen went out for a drive with Princess Henry of Battenberg, and remarked the weather was mild. General Harrison, ex-president of the U.S.A., stood on the deck of the steamer *St Paul*, bound for New York, waving a little square of white handkerchief. His wife remained below. At the precise moment you slid with curled palms on to the cotton sheets of your mother's delivery bed, Prince Frederick Augustus of Saxony fell from his horse and sustained a slight fracture of the skull.'

I didn't laugh. How could I? It might be true. She has such a fertile imagination.

'O darling,' I said, 'darling, what if it were true?'

'Well, it is. Oh yes, and here's a very strange thing. Someone far away in Bohemia or Moravia' (I'm quite sure she had been reading a book on the period) 'was writing a letter to the newspapers saying he was disturbed by the growing amount of anti-semitism. Now if that's not an omen, what is?'

I wrote it all down in my notebook in shorthand, what she had told me. I felt quite unwell. Almost as if I had been present at my own beginnings and if I had only had the knowledge or strength I could have cried out ... 'No, not now ... later. Don't give birth to me now ... it's not fair.' It isn't fair. I should not have been born then. I still have it all in my notebook though I can't read my own writing. She seemed to know a lot more about when I was born than about when she was born. Except the text from the Bible on her day was ... 'And God saw everything he had made and behold it was good.' She wouldn't tell me what my text was. Maybe she genuinely didn't know, but it still worries my mind not knowing and thinking that maybe she knows, and it would be much more enlightening than all that rubbish about the General with his handkerchief, and Augustus falling off his horse.

I asked Claud last night if Maggie had ever told him about the day he was born, but he was too distracted, too depressed suddenly to really concentrate on what poor little me had to say. 'Have another drink,' he said, pouring out more of the dreadful stuff and encouraging me to sing again.

Now that I am sitting in the fresh air, injured though I am, I do begin to remember that there was something dreadfully wrong last night, long before I ran into the china cabinet. A feeling that they were all waiting and expecting something to happen. I did have rather a lot to drink and I was elated by everything around me, but I did feel they were all separately willing a disaster. Norman and Julia were very close, though Norman always does talk to one nose to nose, and she was more animated than I can ever remember. Though I don't know her very well. She did come once with Claud to Morpeth Street, but I think Norman was up his mountains. Oh, the strength of them. The journeys they take, the cars they drive, the mountains they climb.

Claud walked about restlessly and put on a record whose words I could not catch—except something like 'Who's as blue as me ba-a-by'. My head really was tormenting me. Eyes smarting, heart swelling up and up like a brown paper bag, the agony before it splits. I turned my back on them all, hoping they would at least have the decency to notice I was suffering. I felt so lightheaded. There's such a bundle of me always, nothing like the real me at all (though it's only to be expected that I should be all swollen and gorged after an operation such as I had) and I might almost be in disguise. I do wonder whose those stubby little feet belong to, and what trick of light makes my hair look like Flanders wire, and why my teeth have all rotted away, because inside I'm just as I always was, a trim little figure, not thin ever, but firm and shapely and such beautiful glossy hair, and such an air about me of gaiety and flirtatiousness and womanly warmth. And while I sulk behind chairs it's only the big outward me that's showing little white milky teeth, edges sharp as a razor, and I feel so gay.

'What's up, Shebah?' asks Victorian Norman from somewhere in his abrupt way. Don't think I couldn't guess how his hand, hidden from view, was caressing the neck, such a ladylike column of a neck, of Claud's young lady. Maybe Claud knew it too.

'Don't you bloody well know?' I shouted, because I don't have to be polite to Norman, and I was still feeling so pretty and delightful. Friends we are. Friends. Maggie did a painting last winter of the three of us sitting down on the sofa, with the paraffin lamp dangling just above my head. Why she had to put that in I cannot imagine, though there may be some symbolism. It was very clever, the painting, because though she could not have intended to capture it quite so subtly, we all looked so joined together by blobs of paint, so chummily bunched together, and yet on each of the three faces (though it doesn't look in the least like me—and why she had to paint those scarves round my head I don't know) there was such a look of distaste, such enmity in spite of the friendly grouping. And that's how we are really. I despise this so-called friendship and I despise Victorian Norman and his disrespect and I despise Maggie for her so-called kindness, because she never stops picking my brains and taking the credit for it. They are all headed for disaster and they all approach it with such overwhelming *ennui* and lassitude. It hardly matters where I'm heading or in what frame of mind, seeing I was born in 1899 and have received nothing but blows on the head ever since. Claud came round the back of my chair and peered into my face. 'Go away,' I said, flapping at him with my handkerchief, sniffing and yet still smiling at myself, though there was a little gust of irritation beginning to eddy upwards.

'Ah, my love,' he croons, the lying swine, squatting at my feet, so that behind us no doubt Norman and Julia were quite at liberty to do exactly as they wanted.

'An excess of secretion from the lachrymal gland flowing on to the cheek as tears,' said Claud, quite insane, whilst I dabbed at my poor weak eyes, and all the gay cheekiness evaporated slowly, and I felt so angry and so weary. I wanted to hit him. Anyone would have done I suppose—I mean anyone to hit would have done just as well. I don't utterly dislike Claud. He can be kind.

'You're all such fools,' I said. I cannot remember exactly what I said, though I could have bitten my tongue in two afterwards, with regret. I must have said that Maggie really thought him a bloody fool and that she only continued the friendship for all the outings it afforded her and the free drink, and a lot about Norman being after Julia and how Maggie was encouraging him. And after all that, after speaking so indiscreetly and with such malice, though it was the truth, he said so calmly, still sitting at my feet with his fingers still touching the beard for comfort—'Very probably, Shebah ... very probably.' I cannot help myself, I don't want to be disloyal, though God knows they all crucify me ten times a day, but I get so irritated and my words are only a form of vomit. I have no control and no ease till the last little morsel of half-digested hatred is spat into their faces. I sat feeling dreadfully weak then and ashamed, and two moist liquid globes of grief welled up in his eyes and spilled without breaking on to his shirt. I could have died. I couldn't tell him it was an excess secretion from his lachrymal gland or whatever, and I couldn't erase what I had said, but nothing followed the two tears and his eyes dried up and behind us there were scuffling noises and the voice on the record stopped asking 'Who's as blue as me, ba-a-by,' though I might have told him.

'Get up, Shebah,' he said, 'come and look out of the window and smell the air.' He pulled me up out of the chair quite gently and sweetly, though for all I know it might have been then, that singular moment, that he decided to shoot me, when he got the opportunity. Norman and Julia were not in the room. I was quite startled. He didn't seem to notice, just took hold of my hand and drew me to the window, and began clearing the objects from the sill and putting them on the gramophone lid. A little white figure with a parasol and a large silver teapot and an ornate candlestick with a small stuffed bird sitting within its centre cup. The little bird rolled on to the floor when he moved the candlestick and I picked it up for him, such a soft textured creature with minute eyes sewn into the down on either side of its pointed beak. We leaned together on the wide sill overlooking the little yard and the garden beyond. 'Aaah,' I said, taking only little snapping gulps and wishing I could un-say all I had said a moment ago. 'Aaaah,' he breathed, inhaling the cold air and swelling his huge chest. The light from the room shone right on to a tree and made its leaves so green, so lovely. The wistaria curled over the sill we leaned on and he played with its leaves as if they were an extension of his beard. I was worried about Norman and Julia. I hoped they were not out there in the grass beyond the light. I did not want Claud to be made more unhappy, though maybe I don't understand any of them. I asked Claud about Maggie, tentatively this time. I really didn't want to do any more harm. 'Do you think she loves him?' I said, and it was difficult for me, because I had spoken so slightingly about love.

'Not yet,' he said, and turned to look at me, half his face in shadow, and one eye in utter darkness. 'There will,' he continued, and God knows what he meant, and probably it was all words, 'be a worse agony yet to come.'

'But why, darling, why?'

'I can't tell you, Shebah. I only know it to be true. Like a colander spouting a dozen jets, riddled with escaping emotion, Maggie will fall, and Billie, that plap of little pain, will be as nothing.'

'Oh yes, darling,' I said, 'that was dreadful. Poor darling Maggie.' And I meant it. I do mean it. She was unhappy. So excited about him coming home and so hopeful for the future and we all stayed away deliberately and then I met Brenny in the street and hadn't I heard—'Maggie is very ill, and Billie is

157

gone.' Of course, I don't know even now and maybe Claud knows, but he didn't say anything, just kept on fingering the little leaves of the wistaria, but I did hear she tried to kill herself. Imagine, with those two little golden children to care for and all her life in front of her. But it is hard to be certain about Maggie. It's so short a time ago and here she is seemingly none the worse for it and with another devoted lover already breathing her name as if she were a goddess, instead of a sick woman with a divorce on the way and God only knows what else behind her. Nothing seems to check her or break her growth. Any setbacks only serve to accelerate her progress and she laughs quite normally and still has the strength to continue.

'Yes, dreadful,' said Claud.

Oh dear, it's all so dreadful. And so real sometimes. Of course, sitting here now with them all sprawled out on the grass it doesn't seem dreadful at all. They are so resilient. But the air last night, so chill, so cool, and the quiet room so filled with treasures, and the wine inside me and my guilt, and the precise liquid memory of those two realistic unchangeable tears that had spilled so terribly from Claud's eyes, made everything seem so truly without hope. And I almost, yes, almost felt I had crossed the gulf that separated them all from me, because for once I had not merely shared and sympathised with their general suffering but in some way contributed to it. It did not occur to me that it was this factor, this tangling and goading that went on between them, that united them so strongly. They were all partial fashioners of each other's despair, a touch here, a deceit there, words spoken out of turn, hypocrisies, insincerities, insanities binding them like glue and making them in the end indestructible.

I was so busy thinking these thoughts, which are all so much damn rubbish, and worrying my head for answers that I didn't realise Claud too had now gone from the room. Without him at the window it was just another window and I felt cold, so I put all the things back on the ledge and the little brown bird, which reminded me of a song, and I hummed the tune and felt quite clear-headed.

*All through the night there's a little brown bird singing,*
*Singing in the hush of the darkness and the dew....*

Propped against the wall was a painting of a nude woman with long golden hair, and a little dog snuffling in her lap. A very golden painting, though my eyes are half useless. I had to bend down to look at it closely and I half fell over, which made me laugh, and there I was sprawled on the carpet laughing and one of the dogs woke up and pushed its nose into my chest. Really very like the painting. Though the days when I loll about without my clothes are long since past. Not that they ever began. I didn't want Claud to think there was an atmosphere so I began to sing, 'Let's Start All Over Again'. I felt the more noise I made and the more gaiety there seemed to be distilled, the quicker the sadness would be evaporated. And I didn't want anyone to think I was listening to conversations, though everything was very still, and I did not care to think what Victorian Norman was about.

I kept remembering something Maggie had said about Mrs Ryan. How she had gone into her son's room and found a used conservative on the mantelpiece. At the time they all laughed themselves silly over it and I thought they were mad, but I can see now that it's somewhat humorous, though perhaps with spending so much time together, I mean a whole weekend like this, I'm becoming as obsessed as the rest of them. Not that I know for sure what those things look like, though in that house when Eichmann Hanna was bringing his women in every night there were some disgusting things thrown down the toilet. The extremes there are in living. Flushing the toilet in that evil smelling little cubicle and through the broken pane of glass, one star, six-pointed and diamond white, a million light years away, still giving forth such a pure and crystal memory above my weary head.

I got up off the floor and peered out of the window into Claud's sky, but I could not see anything but a multitude of leaves, and whilst I was looking Claud himself came back into the room, as noiselessly as he had left. I did feel better, more naturally gay, and he looked gayer too, more calm, and his eyes though still half barbarous, smiled at me. He is a barbarous man despite his preoccupation with glass and china and everything fragile. A primitive man, half covered in hair, moving about the bejewelled room, humming softly between his two pink lips, picking things up continually, searching with his hands among the pictures and the ornaments for yet more packets of cigarettes and more bottles of wine. Save for the

159

absence of wings he looked like a great furred bee, pushing inside the corolla of a flower, incessantly burrowing for honey. There was still no sign of Julia and I thought I had better sing again to make things easier and whilst I did so Maggie, in a pink-striped nightgown, almost jumped into the room on top of me, with Norman behind her.

'Oh, darling, darling,' I cried, because there was no sign of her birthday Edward and Claud had talked about a worse agony to come, but she certainly did not look agonised, only very peaceful and rosy and rather childish in that striped nightgown. You can never be sure though, for the lighting is so poor and my eyes are so weak, and she might have been upset. She told me that she just felt like a cigarette and wasn't tired and that he, Edward, was asleep. They just don't seem to need sleep. Not tired after a whole day of talking and travelling and dealing with the children and so much wine, and the emotional energy she must have expended during the last hour or so. I simply have not had enough of that sort of experience to know where their energy comes from. Maggie says it's because she recharges herself through her emotional life. I just don't know. Every day I undergo a thousand emotional scenes and yet I never cease to have a feeling of weariness and inertia. Norman and she used to argue about it for hours until my head throbbed exquisitely. She said it was the way in which the energies are directed that determined whether one was refreshed or not. She said that energy was nothing but the instinctual power of sex, which could be sublimated into other useful activities like bathing the baby or painting a picture, but that sooner or later the sublimations would gradually lead to a mood of tiredness. Norman said it was all rubbish, that it was a question of the food we eat, the amount of protein in the diet. I do feel Norman could be right though I despise him so, and he certainly has never bothered to sublimate himself, not for one day. Maggie never used to express herself so clinically until that American came along with his terrible theories. I always knew I was an hysteric, that I had an unstable temperament, thank God, of which I was quite aware before she got hold of all those books on neuroses, but she did tell me that the word hysteria came from the Greek, meaning uterus. It's all so fantastic, so unbelievable, so unpoetic. That little star that shone through that broken pane of glass in that rotting house was unbelievable too, but so pure, so grandly scientific and cosmic, but all this other business is so bound up with bowels and tumours and unpleasant things, and I ought to know because when I had my operation they removed almost everything, including my hysteria too most likely. It did use to be different. There was another mode of living, of courtship, even if I myself never experienced it, it did exist. People had houses and gave dances and hung little lanterns in trees and fragrance billowed outwards when the waltzing began. A man on his knees in the rose pale gravel, clasping a pair of infinitely white gloves to his beseeching breast. A bride going (practically) unkissed with beating heart to her bridegroom's side. Hat, veil and gloves drop to the hotel floor like the petals of a rose. Maggie could never compete in such circumstances. She admits the possibility of a relationship with a man would cause her acute embarrassment if she could not interpret it physically. She never goes walks anywhere. The children are of course a little young. Apart from going up and down the escalators in Lewis's she never seems to take any exercise. To be fair there was a time when she and Norman after midnight would run twice round the Cathedral, but that was nothing but eccentricity.

Ah, the walking I did. My feet were so tantalisingly small, my hair so satisfactorily thick, a great bunch of it hanging down my back. Walking along the promenade, a group of us chattering away, and always such heroic sunsets, and later, not long after, a single star coming out and the wind beginning to blow more strongly, and the feel of my tiny fur collar at the nape of my round neck as I craned my head backwards and stared upwards out of weak eyes, and then suddenly like a firework display the whole sky encrusted with planets and globes and stars and a moon perfectly round, trailing wreaths of vapour and sliding sideways above the black oily river. I won't say it was all beautiful. Some of my so-called friends were dreadful fools. Their banality robbed my heart of heights of happiness. There were times when I felt oppressed by a sense of omission, a feeling that I was utterly alone, that the words I mouthed continually through my unkissed lips were words behind glass and nobody could grasp their meaning. At least not the fools I knew. They made me feel weary all right. Some time I must ask somebody who knows about these things. I never fail to be surprised when I read that great people, great artists, feel exactly as I do. But nobody I actually meet or attempt to communicate with ever feels a damn thing. Perhaps Maggie a little, when she is in a serious frame of mind—between men. Whilst I was curious last night as to why she was not safely tucked up with Edward, I was really more anxious about her and Claud being together. All those deplorable things I had told him. And he really did seem a shade aloof with her. Oh, he smiled and gave her a cigarette and some more to drink, but he went over at once to talk to Norman and left her sitting alone in the armchair. Julia came out of the bedroom, though I cannot remember her going in, and I tried to talk to her. I held her hand for a moment and it was dry and burning, only the polished nails were cool, trapped metallically in my palm. My own hands seemed bloodless and damp by comparison. I said how much Maggie admired Claud (I was lying) and how they understood one another so well.

'Yes, they do, Shebah'—such a polite little voice though it's only the way she shapes her vowels so beautifully, and I began to fear lest I was doing more damage. She is his mistress after all and the relationship between Claud and Maggie is rather strange, and maybe Julia is distrustful anyway. So I just gabbled on, audacious as always, allowing my voice to become a little more contralto, thinking what the hell did it matter anyway as in a very few hours I would be banished from this silver and china room and forgotten in my own hotel, whilst Maggie sat quite still with her eyes closed and a glass in her hand and a meaningless little smile curving her mouth. God knows what she was smiling at. Yet I did have a vague sorrowful emotion in my heart. If I have a heart. Other people of my age (no, I cannot bear it) have hearts that split and wheeze and thunder, necessitating long weeks in bed and an enormous amount of attention. Sweet peas and tender mauve grapes arrive hourly and are placed in colourful heaps on the bedside table. Bunches of daffodils, invalid yellow, are stuck in vases on the window ledges. I cannot stand the anguish of being so without an ailing heart. That that too should be denied me. One day without preliminaries the beating will just stop, the blood stop flowing. No one will guess, let alone enquire. I shall lie frozen for ten days without a heartbeat in an empty house. The forlornness of it.

I half expected Edward to run in and pick up Maggie

without a word and carry her away, and I told Julia as much, but she said she thought he was probably fast asleep, as if she knew out of her own experience that this would be the case. Such a nice girl and very well mannered. We talked about the theatre and about her job before she met Claud, and about Claud's improved health, mental that is, though as far as I can see he's still raving, and about the dogs and the names of all the animals' relations and how when they are in pup you leave them quite alone (I'd leave them alone at all times) and about Maggie. Not very much about Maggie, only she did let slip that Billie had actually come here one Sunday when Maggie was staying for a couple of days. It was only a matter of weeks ago, and they had gone to Julia's parents for a drink and Maggie and he had gone into another room to discuss things.

'What things, darling?'

But she was evasive, perhaps she really didn't know, and she made the observation that Billie appeared to be charming but evidently was not. I did not tell her what I thought of Mr Billie, the rotten swine, talking to me as if I was nobody, always glad to see the back of me, when I had more right, more need to be there than he had. Grudging me a couple of hours in a damp eroded kitchen. I hadn't a large flat to return to, or two devoted parents, or friends and relations sending parcels once a month regularly as clockwork, with home-made plum cake and tins of tobacco, a new pair of socks; just as if he hadn't a large enough salary to buy his own. Why is it that those in receipt of more than their fair share of the vanities of life cannot bear the very poor even a tiny allotment of comfort? When he went away and I used to stay sometimes at Maggie's overnight, in that vast sinful brass bed, with all those poor stuffed animals staring with pebble eyes from each corner of the room, and Victorian Norman banging up and down stairs all night, I used to get such pleasure from thrusting my fist backwards through the head bars of the bed and knocking the photograph of Billie from its nail on the wall just above my pillow. Maggie would mutter from the sofa under the mound of duffle coats and curtains that served her as bedding (I do feel contrite about that) ... 'What's up, Shebah?' and I would reply ... 'Oh God, I don't know, the whole place is like Grand Central Station' ... and think of Billie face downwards with his well-shaped nose full of dust, under the bed on which so many nights he must have lain supreme, whilst I crept like an animal into my hovel round the corner. I didn't really want to stay overnight at Maggie's. There were so many things I ought to have done, my bit of fish to be placed in salted water, my body to attend to, my eye drops, but it was all too much to cope with, and it was always so cold or snowing or blowing a gale and Maggie would say so enticingly—with such warmth—'No, Shebah, dear Shebah, do stay, you can't go back there.' And of course latterly it was just impossible to return there, to even think about it. The house empty, and Eichmann Hanna removed by the authorities and everything falling apart and the gas cut off and the electricity cut off, and the dust and the dirt blowing heedlessly up and down the stairs and the water pouring through the roof and the snow beginning to pile up in the hall. I ask you, what human being could live like that—persecuted by day and night by all the alarms of a battlefield? They just wouldn't believe me when I told them what it was like. And then one night Norman walked me home and I couldn't open the door, and finally when we did enter and Norman shone his torch ... sheet ice from vestibule to roof, a stairway of glass and icicles hanging in petrified ribbons through the rotting banisters. Norman made a little noise, an intake of air, almost a sound of admiration. He stood playing his torch on the whole glacial scene. 'The mind boggles,' he said at last, and took me back to Maggie. After that they were kind to me and I did stay for quite a longish time, but gradually there was a new dimension or rather an old familiar dimension of impatience, and then sly hints and then they began to talk about Rooms to Let in front of me, so that I went out one morning and knocked at the first door that took my demented fancy and booked a room for the following Monday. I did think that their humanity would make them pause and see how impossible it was for me to go on alone, but then Maggie was leaving and Norman was going to take over the ground floor, and no one mentioned the idea of me living in Norman's old room, and how could I ask them? How could I, choking as I was? So I just moved into another little hovel and left all my books and my records and my bits and pieces to rot in that refrigerator along the road. Of course, it did thaw eventually but I hadn't the heart to go back and see all my belongings stained and obliterated and his inscriptions in my books washed out by nature's superhuman tears, and no longer there for me to read. Once I had gone from Maggie's, removed so to speak from the necessity of having my suffering smelling to heaven right under their noses, they were good to me again. My appointments continued as before, and seeing Maggie was only slightly recovering from her traumatic experience of Billie's return and sudden departure, we were not disturbed. There was a difference of course. She seemed very withdrawn and would tell me nothing, absolutely nothing about why she had been ill and what had occurred. I thought she was staying with her mother and then one night I called round to ask Norman if there was any news and there was Maggie passing down the hall, all skin and bone and eyes glittering and a mouth closed in a tight line as if she never intended to speak again. I was so taken aback I said—'Oh, darling, I had no idea ... just pretend I am not here'—and she walked on down the hall and shut the door behind her. I found myself hovering like an anxious moth in the dim hall, not knowing what to do. Norman was no help, he was going out somewhere or other and no, he couldn't talk and no, I shouldn't stay, and yes, Maggie was best left alone, till he almost forced me out of the house into the street and walked off whistling towards the bus stop. A few days later she did send me a little note asking me to call and though she was not her old self (like now) she was grateful for my company. Of course, I was hurt she would not, could not, take me into her confidence. I did so want to understand what had happened to her. Now I realise it was just like everything else; no reason, no depth, meaningless. All she would say to me or to herself were some lines from *Dover Road* (inaccurate, I'm sure):

> *Ah love, let us be true to one another,*
> *For the world that seems to lie before us*
> *Like a land of dreams hath neither hope,*
> *Nor peace, nor certitude ...*

repeating just that over and over like an evocation for help, though how a schoolmaster could understand Maggie and her emotional difficulties, I fail to see. Sometimes a spasm of pain would seize her face, already beginning not to show the bones so prominently, and then she would stew up more tea and busy herself in doing something practical. She did seem to be off men for the time being but then she was packing up and every time I came there were fresh clues to her impending departure. Pictures would be gone from the room, a perfect square of dust outlining their old place on the wall; a stuffed animal sat on a chair in the hall and books in bundles began to climb up the stairs. In the bathroom furniture appeared, freshly painted and covered over with newspaper. The moose that had pointed its antlers above the brass bed lay in the bath, the black tip of its snout resting pensively on the chipped enamel. The Christmas ball that had hung round its neck for years lay in splinters upon the torn lino. It was like visiting a graveyard; the whole house began to assume an air of memory and dedication to the past. Norman walked in and out silently, flowers died in vases, the vases were removed and packed away and the flowers stayed propped up against the wall, cinnamon brown with decay. It was a relief when it ended, when she left on the train for her worse agony to come, as Claud would have it. It was a relief to think that finally my peace, my certitude, my Friday night had seeped away like water down a drain, leaving only debris behind. But then after all I found she had not abandoned me. Victorian Norman has taken up, like a ritual handed down by his Fathers, the ceremony of my Friday night. It's kind or it's cruel. I cannot decide.

I was just about to tell Julia about a play I had been in, when she said she ought to put the kettle on, though that was a lie because I never saw a bloody cup of tea till this morning. When I turned to look at Maggie there was only Victorian Norman sitting in an armchair, legs crossed. No sign of Maggie, no sign of Claud. Gone like the dear dead days beyond recall. There was no use asking Norman for an explanation so we just looked across the carpet at each other, him in his armchair and me on the sofa, heads sunk on our respective breasts, eyeing each other if not with affection, with understanding. 'Ho, ho, my love,' he said insanely, wobbling his foot in its splendour of shiny leather. I did not give him the satisfaction of a reply at which he laughed and closed his eyes and leaned his head back. Not an unpleasant face really, taking it all in all. Perhaps a slight reflection of everyday life, of present-day life. I could just see him pleading for an embrace, mouth gently pursed. Not me, naturally, but some cool efficient girl like Julia. Where have the men gone I wonder? The splendid army captains in their peaked caps with their reckless ways. Norman might have been the hero in some pre-war musical, all wild weak beauty with his foppish hair and his brows arching up like two wings and his well kept hands folded delicately on his lap. Not that he's beautiful by any means. Pathetic rather. Hardly more than a child. Those little orphans that used to go by two by two in Liverpool, listlessly linking hands, dressed in blue, going into the Bluecoat School. A twin back view of plaited hair, a glimpse of marble necks, button boots splashing through the puddles. Maggie squatting earnestly in the back yard in Morpeth Street, the Sunday bells from the Cathedral vibrating through the air, tongue protruding between her teeth, digging with a teaspoon into the sooty soil, planting seeds. 'They will grow, Shebah, you'll see.' And like everything she does, they did, huge perverted sunflowers with faces like Byzantine gongs, struggling Jack and the Beanstalk fashion through the slabs of concrete. Such children, such small and dangerous children. Dear God, how I envy them their childishness. With the ease of pushing with the tongue a piece of food caught in the teeth, they dislodge their miseries and complications. Norman began to snore wildly. With each reverberation his upper lip trembled. A fly landed on his forehead and a vein twitched in protest. He sat up and said to me: 'Where's Julia, Shebah?'

'She's putting the kettle on, darling,' I answered, noting with clarity the little dab of spittle at the corner of his mouth. My eyes seemed to be seeing far more clearly than usual. The leg of the piano, the one nearest to me, was shaped like that of a ballet dancer. Footless it pirouetted and bulged with muscle.

'What's up, old girl?'

Inconceivable he should be talking to me. Old girl of mine, old pal of mine, I'm weary and lonely it's true.... When I did not reply he stood up and stretched himself and went meekly downstairs, passing under the wooden angel. Like a stage direction for some Shaksperian play (another part of the wood) Edward moved through the room in pyjamas, a dressing gown of gaudiness dragging across the carpet. We did not speak. He looked out of the window and went almost at once into the bathroom. A long pause. Water gurgling into the basin. They fly in search of repose trembled on the edge of a crystal drop of sheer glass that swayed under its weight. Edward crossed the carpet again, trailing clouds of glory, smoking his cigarette. He flicked a little mound of ash tidily into the hearth and crossed back again to the window. A clearing of the throat.

'A lovely night.'

'Yes, dear, a lovely night.'

Such children in their observations, their ability to be articulate about the obvious. I felt overdressed not being in night attire. The door downstairs opened. The alarm bell shattered the room; with a faint hum of irritation the fly rose in the air and spun under the ceiling. With a sense of purpose, God bless him, Edward went to the head of the stairs and stood with folded arms. A sob or perhaps a laugh from halfway down and then Maggie with chilled shoulders and remote face appearing like an apparition, not quite in focus. Edward went into the guest room and Maggie followed. Pretend I am not here, I might have said; there was no need, she was not aware of me. One of the most, the most disheartening things about all this coming and going and change your partners and weekends in the country, is that there is no one, no one at all, to whom I can unfold this tale in all its magnitude. I simply would not be believed. Or comprehended. It would be casting pearls before swine. I suppose I might drop it to Mrs Malvolio that I spent the weekend in an antique shop. The marvels hanging on the walls, the dear blue china plates rolling round the shelves. The praying angel would be appreciated. But can I possibly repeat that most of the guests spent half the night wandering about in night attire, that the host let fall two oval tears upon his checked shirt? Before the ending of the night a hundred pounds of damage done and at dawn a bullet, whining like a bee, sped to my palpitating flesh. Face down among the daisies, nearer O Lord to Thee. 'Shot?' says Mrs Malvolio, Catholic face empurpled. 'Accidentally, of course?'

'No, with intent, by a friend, ballistically at dawn.'

Such a pity it cannot be enacted.

No sooner had Maggie and Edward removed themselves than Claud arrived halfway up the stairs, unclothed it seemed. The bare breasts came into view, nipples like raisins embedded in the white flesh.

'Claud, darling,' I screamed, not that I truly cared if the whole damn lot ran stark naked.

'It's all right, my love, I have my lower garments.'

He had, he explained, been attending to his roses outside. Julia and Norman (where had they been?) lay down behind the sofa and began to pluck at a harp that lay on its side. I did think foolishly that she was waiting for the kettle to boil, otherwise I should have gone to bed. I would have gone to bed.

I cannot allow myself to dwell on what happened later. Those little broken figures and the pieces of glass shining like tears on the carpet. It was an accident. I am not usually accident prone nor predisposed to being clumsy. With what shame and remorse, with burning face and throbbing head, I retired to bed.

'Good night, darlings ... O darlings.'

'Good night, my love.'

'Good night, Shebah.'

'Sleep well, my dove.'

I did not really sleep. I was too confused and the children made little worrying sounds in their slumber. This morning, at least before my execution, Claud was very kind, very generous. Without suspicion, trustingly, I rose and cleaned my face and went out into the garden among the roses and the trees. The head of Edward wavered between two branches and a cloud of leaves. A bird sang and the sun shone palely overhead. When I was shot I distinctly heard Victorian Norman laughing. God forgive him.

Not such a surprising occasion after all. Have I not been reviled, cursed, wounded, all my life? Did not Prince Augustus of Saxony sustain a fracture of the skull, the moment I was born?

The monotony of it all. Whilst they lie indolent in the sun, unaware of their worse agonies to come, I wait with closed eyes.

For something, someone ... for two great and gentle hands to lift me from my cross ... for anything ...

'Betty,' repeated Stanley. He was angry and a little unhappy. She put down the photograph at once on to the smooth plush face of the sofa and rose to her feet, smoothing her skirt down with her hands. 'Yes, of course, dear, I'm so sorry. What time is it?'

'Gone one, and I've a meeting at three.' He turned in a businesslike way to Claud and held out his hand. 'It's been very pleasant meeting you, Mr White. May I ask if I get a van to fetch my desk or do you manage that side of it?' He made to disengage his hand but Claud held it firmly.

'Well, as a general rule I let my customers make their own arrangements,' said Claud, 'but you live quite near and it will be no trouble to deliver it personally. Sometime next week, maybe Monday or Tuesday. Tuesday most like, man.'

'Oh, that's very good of you. Much obliged.' This time Stanley succeeded in removing his fingers from Claud's grip and resolutely he tried not to notice that it was his wife Claud was watching. It was too absurd to think about. Not Betty. She just wasn't the type. He shook his head almost smiling and Betty and he went down the stairs into the shop, followed by Claud and Julia.

'Do come again sometime,' invited Julia vaguely. She leaned against Claud in the doorway and watched the couple get into their car. It was a big shiny car and there was a fluffy animal dangling from a string, visible through the rear window.

The woman Betty did not look in their direction. She bent her head as if looking for something and the car drove off up the street. When they had gone Julia went straight into the kitchen and began to attend to the child's nappies. Claud bent down by the sink and put his hand into the wastage bucket.

'What on earth are you doing?'

'There's that fellow's cheque in here somewhere.' He straightened up empty-handed.

'His cheque?'

'Mmm. You swept it up, my love. It's there somewhere. Do look for it, Ju, when you've a moment.'

He wiped his hand on the side of his trousers and went out and through the door into the yard. There were small flecks of soot spotting the surface of the pillow in the pram. How upset Julia would be. He stood looking at the barn for a long moment. He would take the desk up in two weeks' time, not one. He would put his arm about the woman Betty and get her to confide in him. He would call upon her quite regularly and do no more than kiss her, ever. He would make her life richer, more articulated. He entered the barn and walked along its length till he came to the green sofa and sat down upon it. When Julia had come to save him he had been too ill to make love to her. She had handled him like a sick child and had been surprised when finally one afternoon he had lain her down on the green sofa and taken her.

'But, darling,' she had protested, 'someone might see us through that little wondow.'

'Yes, I know,' he told her, pushing her down into the warmth of the sofa and laying his cheek against her damp skin. No one had seen them because no one could see through the little window; the glass was too dim and the creeper that climbed about the barn was too thick. In parts the creeper had burst through the roof. It meant the rain came through as well but the effect was worth the slight damage done. He stroked the sofa tenderly with his fingers and let his chin sink on to his chest. Then he remembered the letter still in his pocket. He took it out and read it through once, twice ...


'Dear Flower,

Could you send the photograph you took in the garden? It's urgent. I don't think Edward wants to marry me after all. Actually it doesn't really matter because I'm not pregnant now, though I don't think I'll tell him. I did tell him I was a couple of weeks after we left you and he was awfully nice but I don't think he likes me very much now. I can sort of tell. I don't particularly want to marry him either but I would like a chance to refuse, if you know what I mean. Only thing is I think he'll try and get a job somewhere just to get away. Still I am very cheerful love. How are you and Julia? Norman says he tried in the barn but Julia wasn't having any. I want the photo just to show Edward. If it's a pretty one of me, I mean if I look quite nice, maybe he'll love me again. Please don't forget. Norman says Shebah wore her bandage for weeks, till it fell off with filth. Are you happy? If Edward does go away I shall just live a sensible normal life—no more messes or intrigues. This time I mean it. Don't laugh. Have you read a man called Wallace Stevens?

> *There is or may be a time of Innocence,*
> *There is never a place. Or if there is no time*
> *If it is not a thing of time, nor of place . . .*

and something and something. There's a lot more like that. He used to go up and down and up and down in lifts in America. Please take care. You could light a candle for me. Blessings. M.'

Claud read the lines of verse several times without making much sense of them. He decided she's probably remembered it wrongly or disordered the punctuation. He folded the letter very carefully and rose from his seat and went to the newly bought desk. Opening the right-hand drawer he thrust the letter into the darkness for Betty to find and to read.

He would sometime send Maggie the photograph, even if it was a year late and Edward had long since departed. Maybe the loved one of the moment would pause in flight and rediscover a new and more desirable Maggie staring up at him from the grass. He went into the house again and up the stairs into the living room. He picked up the photograph from off the sofa and propped it on the mantelpiece before going into the bedroom to look for an envelope. Through the window he noticed the cat from next door move across the yard and lose itself in the long grass of the little garden. The miniature tiger stalked through its miniature jungle, unseen.

Sucking threads of beard in at the crinkled corners of his pink mouth, he went downstairs to cut the grass.

The photograph remained on the mantelpiece for a long time. It accumulated dust and was bent at one corner. The four people posed on, staring outwards into the crowded room.

On the right-hand side there were the three friends, two of them reclining and the third sitting uncomfortably on a white cane chair, skirt stretched tight over swelling thighs. There were roses not yet in bloom, and a tree, some sort of a tree, bending down with a branch almost touching the ground, and behind four statues with bowed heads and folded hands. On the left, isolated, hunched so that black hair jutted out over his collar, was the fourth figure, eyes small against the sun.

Missing were the daisies sewed tight in the grass, so little, so white, and the exquisite line of dust on Shebah's hat, shone on by the sun.

All of them silent, marooned in private contemplation, waiting for a moment of departure under the unblown roses.

Panther Fiction

# THE GIRLS   25p

## Nicola Thorne

Jacoba is mature, emancipated, far too wise
to get pregnant.
Honey and Pauline are silly dollies who share
a bedroom—and a desire for older men.
Bea is the brainy one: she loses her religion
along with her virginity, and feels better
for both.
The Beauty is a luscious model who allows the
occasional male to ruffle her sheets but not
her complexion.
And they all live together in Morag's little
house on April Avenue

# I JAN CREMER  48p

## Jan Cremer

This autobiographical novel is the
authentic expression of one aspect of the
tumultuous nineteen-sixties, written by a
young Dutch author who, in his own
words is: 'Nervous, schizophrenic,
frustrated, sadistic, perverted, sexually
abnormal, an inspirer of riots, a committer
of bestialities.' This roaring, raucous story
of Jan Cremer's swing through Europe
and the United States certainly epitomises
all the multitudinous aspects of
Mr. Cremer's fragmented personality

## SOME PANTHER AUTHORS

Norman Mailer
Jean-Paul Sartre
Len Deighton
Henry Miller
Georgette Heyer
Mordecai Richler
Gerard de Nerval
James Hadley Chase
Juvenal
Violette Leduc
Agnar Mykle
Isaac Asimov
Doris Lessing
Ivan Turgenev
Maureen Duffy
Nicholas Monsarrat
Fernando Henriques
B. S. Johnson
Edmund Wilson
Olivia Manning
Julian Mitchell
Christopher Hill

Robert Musil
Ivy Compton-Burnett
Chester Himes
Chaucer
Alan Williams
Oscar Lewis
Jean Genet
H. P. Lovecraft
Anthony Trollope
Robert van Gulik
Louis Auchincloss
Vladimir Nabokov
Colin Spencer
Alex Comfort
John Barth
Rachel Carson
Simon Raven
Roger Peyrefitte
J. G. Ballard
Mary McCarthy
Kurt Vonnegut
Alexis Lykiard